# PARENT EDUCATION AND
# ELEMENTARY COUNSELING

New Vistas in Counseling Series
*Series Editors*—Garry Walz and Libby Benjamin
*In collaboration with ERIC Counseling and Personnel Services Information Center*

**Structured Groups for Facilitating Development: Acquiring Life Skills, Resolving Life Themes, and Making Life Transitions, Volume 1**
Drum, D. J., Ph.D. and Knott, J. E., Ph.D.

**New Methods for Delivering Human Services, Volume 2**
Jones, G. B., Ph.D., Dayton, C., Ph.D. and Gelatt, H. B., Ph.D.

**Systems Change Strategies in Educational Settings, Volume 3**
Arends, R. I., Ph.D. and Arends, J. H., Ph.D.

**Counseling Older Persons: Careers, Retirement, Dying, Volume 4**
Sinick, D., Ph.D.

**Parent Education and Elementary Counseling, Volume 5**
Lamb, J. and Lamb, W., Ph.D.

**Counseling in Correctional Environments, Volume 6**
Bennett, L. A., Ph.D., Rosenbaum, T. S., Ph.D. and McCullough, W. R., Ph.D.

**Transcultural Counseling: Needs, Programs and Techniques, Volume 7**
Walz, G., Ph.D., Benjamin, L., Ph.D., et al.

**Career Resource Centers, Volume 8**
Meerbach, J., Ph.D.

**Behavior Modification Handbook for Helping Professionals, Volume 9**
Mehrabian, A., Ph.D.

WITHDRAWN

# PARENT EDUCATION AND ELEMENTARY COUNSELING

**Jackie Lamb,** *M.Ed.*
*American College Testing Service,*
*Iowa City*

**Wesley A. Lamb,** *Ph.D.*
*Illinois Department of Mental*
*Health*

*Vol. 5 in the New Vistas in Counseling Series,*
*in collaboration with*
*ERIC Counseling and Personnel Services*
*Information Center*
*Series Editors—Garry Walz and Libby Benjamin*

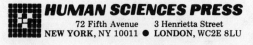
**HUMAN SCIENCES PRESS**
72 Fifth Avenue    3 Henrietta Street
NEW YORK, NY 10011 ● LONDON, WC2E 8LU

Library of Congress Catalog Number 77-12942
ISBN: 0-87705-318-9

Copyright © 1978 Human Sciences Press
72 Fifth Avenue, New York, N.Y. 10011

Printed in the United States of America
89 987654321

**Library of Congress Cataloging in Publication Data**

Lamb, Jackie.
    Parent education and elementary counseling.

    (New vistas in counseling; v. 5)
    Includes bibliographical references.
    1. Personnel service in elementary education.
2. Children—Management—Study and teaching.
I. Lamb, Wesley A., joint author.  II. Title.
III. Series.
LB1027.5.L28      372.1'4      77-12942
ISBN 0-87705-318-9

# CONTENTS

# FOREWORD

All of us have had parents of one sort or another, many of us are parents, and a large number of us can expect to be parents at some time in our lives—a simple reality that has existed since man and woman first came to be. Curious, isn't it, that while formal education concerns itself with the development of intellectual skills and cognitive processes, it has not attended to preparing young people for a life role that nearly all of them will assume within just a few years after leaving school. If, indeed, the way we deal with our children reflects our own upbringing, then learning to be a good parent has profound implication for the kind of society that will emerge in the future.

Increasingly, we in the helping professions are realizing that the best "medicine" is preventive—before the fact, before the problems occur, before situations requiring rehabilitation or treatment develop. Consultants and helping professionals, recognizing that a troubled child exemplifies a troubled environment, work with school personnel and parents to remedy the child's world. Teachers, too, especially at the elementary level, reach beyond the educational setting, and within severe time constraints do what they can, by themselves or through referrals, to help remedy difficult family situations. Training for effective parenting has mushroomed in the form of workshops, continuing education courses, and agency-sponsored programs, clear evidence that the need to learn to be a good parent is critical.

While we advocate that parenting skills are best taught before one becomes a parent, we also recognize that most parents have not had training in child-rearing and that counselors must be equipped to help parents in their quest to perform their roles adequately or better. Thus, we at ERIC/CAPS commissioned Jackie and Wesley Lamb to share their knowledge and expertise in a publication that would do just that. Bringing together into one volume the work of a number of theorists, the authors describe not only the basic rationale and goals of each approach but also procedures and strategies counselors may use to implement the approach. They also include useful hints for start-up and tips on evaluation that will help the counselor assess outcomes from the chosen intervention. The result, we believe, is a document that maintains and enriches our policy of generating resources that go beyond theory and are of immediate and practical use to counselors in their work settings.

Garry R. Walz and Libby Benjamin
Director and Associate Director, ERIC/CAPS

# PREFACE

The goals of this monograph are basically practical. We do not intend to develop an extremely scholarly presentation and analysis of all of the material on parent education. We do intend, however, to provide the elementary counselor and other interested professionals with some basic information about several models of parent training. In addition to this basic information which can be viewed as primarily an overview, we hope to provide some practical considerations which will be of assistance to professionals instituting parent education or parent counseling programs at the local level. We also include a bibliography at the end of each section that will provide further information specific to a given model.

No counselor or other pupil personnel specialist should be expected to be competent to carry out a program of parent education on the basis of this monograph alone. We are assuming that all persons setting up parent education programs will have had appropriate professional training in some of the skills that are seen as prerequisites to participation in a counseling program. Various models of counseling disagree as to the nature of the basic skills, and we make no attempt to determine what they should be for a given counselor in a given setting. We do assume that some type of training program has certified or will certify that the counselor has at least rudimentary skills.

We follow as much as possible the same outline or presentation with each of the models of parent education. This outline is as follows:

1.  History
2.  Basic Assumptions
3.  Goals
4.  Training Procedures
5.  Training of Trainers
6.  References and Resources

The history, basic assumptions and goals of each of the major models of parent education are presented so that parent educators or prospective parent educators can determine the model that best fits their personal styles and best meets the needs of their particular settings. In this manner, the parent educator can operate as a more informed consumer of theories and training procedures.

The primary exception to this outline involves the section dealing with training of trainers. Very few of the models give specifics on this point, resulting in gaps in the outline. These gaps represent deficiencies in the literature.

The chapter titled "Guide for Getting Going" deals with issues that arise when a parent education program is started. These are issues that need to be considered by every parent educator regardless of theoretical orientation. Our general suggestions for parent educators are included in this section. Suggestions relating to specific models of parent education are presented at the time the model is reviewed.

*Chapter 1*

# INTRODUCTION

## DEFINITION OF PARENT EDUCATION

Prior to the review of models and techniques of parent training, some type of consensus on the definition of the term "parent training" must be reached. We are aware of the complexity and difficulty of the various tasks of being a parent. For the purposes of this monograph, we use a broad definition of "parenting" that covers all responses, activities, and skills involved in child management, child rearing, parent-child communications, and general care of a child. We are well aware that this definition is vague. We are also aware that parenting skills are clearly a function of a number of variables such as innate and reflexive responses, social and personal values, environmental circumstances and a multitude of less obvious variables.

Since we are unable to define parenting even to our own satisfaction, we are hesitant to define "education" or "training" (the terms will be used synonomously through this monograph). We shall proceed with a simple definition of parent education: the formal attempt to increase parents' awareness and facility with the skills of parenting.

One might well ask why anyone would attempt to influence such a complex "natural" skill as parenting. One response to such an inquiry is an analogy used by Lamb and Reidy (1975) comparing the complex tasks of parenting and speaking. Most people, barring some type of special situation, learn to parent. The same could be said of speaking. But listening to those around us as well as to ourselves confirms the opinion that some people are clearly better speakers than others. There are a number of articulatory errors, repetitions, substitutions, distortions, dysfluencies, and other difficulties demonstrated in speaking. With a task as complex as speaking, various degrees of these problems as well as particular skills can be observed in each individual. The complex task of parenting is similar since we can observe particular skills or lack of skills.

When particular deficits in speech are identified, services are available in many community agencies such as schools for the remediation of the problem. Screening projects are often instituted to identify children eary so that they can start to develop within the normal or acceptable range. In addition to individual remediation programs, we often find speech and language development programs provided for all members of a group. Such programs are often viewed as a means of facilitating development as well as serving a preventive function.

Parent training has similar goals. Increasing parenting skills in members of the community, early identification of those with particular needs, and the remediation of identified problems are the general goals of all references reviewed for this monograph. Professionals working with children and families have in fact identified areas of parental functioning that appear to be related to children's functioning. These professionals have accepted the role of intervening in a situation to increase the level of parental functioning in specific parents and in the broader community of parents.

Caplan (1964) speaks of the various types of prevention of mental illness. Caplan's model of primary, secondary, and tertiary prevention can be applied to the general area of professionals working with parents. Most interventions directly involving parents in the mental health of their children focus on dealing with the parents of children who have been identified as having particular mental health problems. Working with identified problems is tertiary prevention. Some programs in mental health focus on working with parents in the early identification of their children's mental health problems. These projects fit into the level of secondary prevention. Primary prevention projects involve parents in preventing mental health problems. Our review of the literature identifies very few attempts to provide primary prevention. The three exceptions to this deficit are found in affective education (Cottingham, 1973), elementary counseling with a developmental focus (Lamb and Deschenes, 1973), and the parent training movement that has had periods of growth and decline over the last 90 years (Brim, 1959).

## DISTINCTION BETWEEN PARENT TRAINING AND THERAPY

The goals of therapy and training are similar and overlap in some areas, but there is a distinction between them. The distinction is as important for parents as it is for the professionals providing both services. Lamb and Reidy (1975) present the following table to delineate this distinction:

| *Parent training is:* | *Parent training is not:* |
|---|---|
| 1. training in child management | 1. parent psychotherapy |
| 2. study of issues involved in normal child development | 2. marital counseling |
| 3. training in communication skills and communication analysis | 3. primarily a way of helping the parents relive their own childhood |
| 4. based on the assumption that specific skills are related to being a "better" parent | 4. a place for parents to complain about their children and "kids today" |
| 5. time limited and usually short term | 5. long term and expensive |
| 6. task oriented | 6. person and relationship oriented |

Therapy typically focuses on the affective domain while education and training work with the cognitive. Therapy usually implies an existing internalized problem; training does not. There are, of course, parent trainers and therapists or counselors who would disagree with some of these distinctions. It is important for counselors and parents to clarify the goals and procedures of both training and therapy. Both parties to the implied contract between parent and trainer or parent and therapist must agree on goals, procedures and values.

Christensen (1969) suggests that parents be viewed as people who need to learn and not people who are sick. Since they need to learn, education and not therapy is the most appropriate approach. If one agrees with this position, it is entirely fitting for school professionals to include parent education in their programs.

## HISTORY OF PARENT TRAINING

Historically, it can be assumed that the first parent training in the human race was children's observation of their parents engaged in the complex skills of parenting. Training was informal and accomplished by means of children identifying with, modeling on, and imitating significant parenting adults in their environment. We can further assume that the first attempt at formal parent training took place after humans developed sufficient communication skills for grandparents (or other members of the group) to give suggestions to their children concerning the raising of grandchildren.

From this rudimentary beginning, parent training progressed through the ancient Greek and Roman sages, who commented astutely on the rearing of future citizens. Our first reference with direct relevance to contemporary parent training is *Education for Child Rearing* by Brim (1959). Brim's history of parent training indicates that even though there were apparently active parent training programs in Europe during the 18th century, interest in this country came into focus during the early part of the 19th century. Brim notes that several magazines appeared between 1830 and 1850 (*Mother's Magazine, Mother's Assistant,* and *Parent's Magazine*) which evidence interest during this period. He cites other writers interested in the history of parent training who have traced group meetings of parents in America as early as 1815 and "maternal associations" meeting throughout the country around 1820. He identifies the Child Study Association of America, founded in 1888 as the Society for the Study of Child Nature, as the oldest United States group with a continuing parent education focus. The National Congress of Parents and Teachers, founded around the beginning of the twentieth century as the Congress of Mothers, had as an express purpose educating parents in child development. The years between 1920 and the early 1930's, Brim notes, were particularly active. During this period various programs sprang up, and parent education became professionalized due to the availability of private and government monies. Sources of funding diminished in the middle to late 1930's, and the field suffered a setback in professional activities. Brim's work includes a list of 36 national organizations which specify parent education as a goal.

This brief history from Brim's work is presented to give a perspective on the field of parent training-parent education which indicates that even though a number of counselors, counselor educators, pupil personnel specialists, and other social and personal interveners feel they are creating a new field when they deal with parent training, they are in error. Others have been there previously.

## RATIONALE FOR PARENT TRAINING

Part of the rationale for parent training is illustrated by the previous analogy between speaking and parenting. Professionals and others responsible for the well-being and development of children have taken it upon themselves to engage in various levels of prevention of mental disorders much the way other responsible child agents have dealt with issues of speech and language development. In a sense, the movement of counselors into the area of parent training is entirely consistent with the emphasis on child advocacy proposed by the White House Conference on Children and Youth, 1970.

Waggoner (1970), in his presidential address to the American Psychiatric Association, gave several recommendations to his colleagues regarding preventive psychiatry. Two dealt directly with parent training. He suggested developing a training program for potential parents in high school and college, and establishing counseling centers for parents seeking advice.

Several writers take the position that working with parents is an appropriate function for counselors. Lamb and Deschenes (1973) make this point when outlining the role of elementary school counselors. McGehearty (1968) expounds on the position that counselors would be spending their time much more efficiently by dealing with the caretakers of children rather than with the individual children who appear to have the most severe problems. The position is essentially one of pragmatics—using counselors in tasks where they can perform the greatest good for the greatest number. In his position paper on the direction of counseling in the 1980's, Berdie (1972) suggests counselors start working as applied behavioral scientists, facilitating individual development by working with a focus larger than just one child. Working with students, parents, families, teachers and administrators would help provide experiences to promote individual development.

Rheingold (1973), a specialist in child development, takes the position that up until now psychologists (and specialists in behavioral sciences) have given little practical assistance to parents. Many studies are presented in the literature but little if any assistance is offered in response to the question, "What can you tell me about raising my children so that they have a better chance of growing up without problems and of reaching their potential?" Rheingold holds that enough information is now available to answer this and similar questions, and she encourages professionals to accept responsibility in this area.

More than twenty years ago Gruenberg (1952) addressed several issues of parent training. Even at that time parents were being bombarded with conflicting advice about raising children. According to Gruenberg's prediction, parents would look to the school for collaboration in child development and is establishing a higher quality relationship between parents and children. Gruenberg suggested that schools assume a joint responsibility in this process rather than fear that by engaging in such activities they are taking away the responsibility of the parents.

Even teachers are suggesting that elementary school counselors should have more contacts with parents, according to Masih (1969). Teachers surveyed felt that counselors should see parents individually and in groups and should spend more time following up cases with teacher and parent contacts.

Hanson (1968) found that 92% of the parents surveyed felt that the counselor could expect to have the parent and child follow through on plans agreed to by all three parties. This implies a close working relationship among the three parties which is not limited to parent training but could become a crucial aspect of it.

Garner and Sperry (1968) completed a survey of approximately 500 mothers of children in grades one through six to find out: (1) sources of child care information and services; (2) types of information and services they receive; (3) types of services they need. The majority of mothers indicated that they received most of their information from family and friends. Approximately one-third indicated that they needed more information on school and education. Approximately half of the mothers indicated that discussion groups would be the preferred means of obtaining such information and services. These findings indicate that services in the school program could be added or expanded to meet these needs.

Another rationale for parent training is found in research literature which indicates such training is beneficial. The amount of research on the effectiveness of parent training is extremely small, considering the amount of attention given the area currently and in the past. Like most areas in which child advocates and social interveners are working, little attention has been given to evaluation of the intervention. References giving empirical demonstration of effectiveness are presented later in the monograph under the type of theoretical model appropriate for the training used.

Data presented by Pigott (1969) provide a brief example of an empirical rationale derived from an experiment. Fifty underachieving boys and girls were the subject of this study. The children's parents saw counselors for fifteen weekly half-hour sessions. Fifty-four percent of the experimental group improved, 23% remained the same, and 23% regressed. In the control group only 19% gained, while 30% stayed the same, and 50% went down in performance. Accordingly, Pigott concludes that the approach was effective.

Thus, several major rationales can be seen for the provision of parent training services (the first three are from the prevention of mental illness model described by Caplan):

1. helping parents intervene when their child shows signs of emotional disturbance.

2. helping parents recognize early signs of emotional disturbance so that early intervention is possible.

3. helping change environmental situations and stresses so that emotional disturbances in children are less likely to occur.

4. various professionals and specialists agree that there are sufficient information and skills available now that relate to assisting parents in helping children to develop as fully as possible.

5. teachers are suggesting that counselors become involved in this area.

6. parents indicate that they desire information on child development and their role in this development.

7. studies indicate that parent training is effective.

8. parental involvement is good public relations policy in a number of areas.

9. working with the parents as well as the child gives the counselor a better picture of the child's total environment.

10.   there is evidence that work with parents brings about better results than work with child as the only target.

11.   working with parents fits well with the current focus of counselors spending more time in "consultation" rather than in direct contact with children.

# REFERENCES

Berdie, R. F. The 1980 counselor: Applied behavioral scientist. *Personnel and Guidance Journal,* 1972, **50,** 451–456.

Brim, O. G. *Education for child rearing.* New York: Russell Sage Foundation, 1959.

Caplan, G. *Principles of preventive psychiatry.* New York: Basic Books, 1964.

The Chicago Association for Child Study and Parent Education. *Intelligent parenthood.* Chicago: The University of Chicago Press, 1926.

Christensen, O. C. Education: A model for counseling in the elementary school. *Elementary School Guidance and Counseling Journal,* 1969, **4,** 12–19.

Cottingham, H. F. Psychological education, the guidance function, and the school counselor. *The School Counselor,* 1973, **20,** 340–345.

Garner, K. B., & Sperry, I. N. *Information and services obtained and devised by parents of elementary school children.* Greensboro: University of North Carolina, 1968.

Gruenberg, S. M. *Our children today.* New York: The Viking Press, 1952.

Hanson, E. B. Middle class parents look at the role and function of counselor. *The School Counselor,* 1968, **16,** 115–119.

Lamb, J., & Deschenes, R. The unique role of the elementary counselor. *Elementary School Guidance and Counseling Journal,* 1973, **8,** 219–223.

Lamb, W. A., & Reidy, T. J. *The SOAP system: A proposed model for parent training.* Unpublished manuscript, DePaul University, 1975.

Masih, L. K. Elementary school teachers view elementary counseling. *The School Counselor,* 1969, **17,** 105–107.

McGehearty, L. The case for consultation. *Personnel and Guidance Journal,* 1968, **47,** 257–326.

Pigott, K. M. *Parent counseling and academic achievement: Progress report on the initiation of a system-wide parental consultation program.* Paper presented at the APGA Convention, Las Vegas, 1969. (ERIC Document Reproduction Service No. ED 058 572).

Rheingold, H. L. To rear a child. *American Psychologist,* 1973, **28,** 42–46.

Waggoner, R. W. The presidential address: Cultural dissonance and psychiatry. *American Journal of Psychiatry,* 1970, **12**(1), 1–8.

Logical and natural consequences? Family meetings or councils? Encouragement? These may be new terms, but they are essential to counselors using Adlerian methods in parent-education progams Teaching parents how to have "democratic living" in the home is one of the most important lessons in this model. To accomplish the goal of democratic living parents learn how to ecnourage their children, to relate to children on an equal basis, to use logical and natural consequences more effectively and to understand the goals of children's misbehavior.

*Chapter 2*

# ADLERIAN PARENT EDUCATION

## HISTORY

Alfred Adler devised this methodology in the early 1900's when he published his defense of the current work on dream interpretation. The article brought him and Freud together, and in 1902 Adler joined the Vienna Psychoanalytic Society. Adler's main interest and concentration were in over-compensation. His views on organ inferiority and compensation were first published in 1907. As time went on he became more interested in the psychological and subjective reasons for man's behavior. After World War I he spent his time organizing child guidance centers which had great impact on education.

Adler worked at a time when parents and educators were greatly influenced by Freud and his followers. Parents were feeling confused by differences between traditional methods of raising children and new ideas being offered by Freud. All in all this seems to have made for a time when parents were raising children without a definite, consistent set of guidelines or patterns. Due to the resulting confusion in parents' thinking, there was much "hopping" between the new and the old approaches (Dreikurs & Grey, 1968; Watson, 1963).

In the late 1920's and early 1930's Adler became known in the United States. Perhaps the greatest stronghold for his teachings was the Chicago Guidance Center, later known as The Alfred Adler Institute, which was started by Dr. Rudolph Dreikurs. Until his death a few years ago Dreikurs had a major impact on counselors and parent educators.

## Basic Assumptions

Some of Adler's principles particularly pertinent to children and parents are discussed by Dreikurs, Corsini, Lowe, and Sonstegard (1959); Dreikurs and Grey (1968); Dreikurs, Gould, and Corsini (1974); and Watson (1963). A summary of these principles follows:

1. Man is a social being; even the young seek ways to be part of the family and other groups.

2. Humans want to be socialized; therefore, their social interest becomes the most important facet of their striving.

3. All behavior is purposive; man is a goal seeking organism. To understand behavior and actions, you must know the goals.

4. Each person creates a life style which is a sum total of the attitudes, goals, and beliefs he/she develops to find his/her place or achieve his/her goal.

5. The law of equality on which our society is based demands recognition of everyone as an equal.

6. With freedom comes responsibility.

7.   Cooperation is needed between family members, not permissiveness. Cooperation cannot happen without accepting responsibility.

8.   Infants operate by trial and error and begin to discriminate sets of responses. They learn to avoid pain and punishment and to give responses which bring them satisfaction. By four to six years of age, they have formed a concept of how they can find their place in the family.

9.   We behave in accordance with our expectations.

Attempts have been made to build a more democratic society on the principle of equality. The upheaval of the 1960's and 1970's was due in part to the denial of equality to certain members of society. No longer will women, non-whites or the young accept second class citizenship. Many traditions, rules and guidelines are no longer accepted; they are challenged and so must bend and change. Children openly question parents' authority. People are bombarded by facts, figures and statistics which say the young are causing trouble for others and for themselves. Could the problem be that children have freedom but not equality? Could it be that parents are frustrated because they are told to "buckle down" and "tighten up," while at the same time they see that the old authoritarianism isn't working?

Elementary schools are plagued with reluctant learners, children who are unwilling to cooperate at learning. New teaching materials and methodologies are used, but many of the same problems still exist. Counseling has been included in the elementary school since approximately 1965 in order to provide children with an advocate in the system. With this development it is increasingly clear that we must work with the significant adults in a child's life (Christiansen, 1969; Dinkmeyer, 1973a; Lamb & Deschenes, 1973). Since parents are recognized as an important resource to professionals working with children, it is important that parents be offered assistance and education in the skills of parenting. Parent education can be offered as part of the on-going school counseling program to help parents do a more effective job of raising their children and to increase communication between home and school.

## Goals

According to Dreikurs et al. (1959) the " philosophy of parent education is to do unto others as you would have others do unto you." Since parents follow the examples of their parents before them, re-education is needed. We must help parents become educators. One of the goals then is to help parents understand children, to know how they think and to comprehend the motives for their actions. Another goal is to help parents improve the quality of help they provide their children. Perhaps the goal of goals is to help parents relate more effectively to their children (Dinkmeyer, 1968b).

In Adlerian family counseling (family counseling is the most common model of Adlerian parent education), the overall goals are general; however, the goals each family sets for itself are very specific. The general goals were mentioned above; examples of specific goals follow:

1.  Reduce the number of fights between the children by making sure mother or dad does not become involved.
2.  Each person is responsible for his or her own room and belongings and therefore mother does not pick up after anyone.
3.  All members share work chores on a rotating basis, even the baby.

Since goals for each family are concrete, changes in family patterns are observable. It would be easy to observe any of the three goals mentioned above.

The family has 100% responsibility for selection of goals. The counselor offers suggestions such as, "How would it be if this week no one is called by mom or dad to get ready for school?" If the parents are uncomfortable with allowing the children to be late, another goal would be suggested or this one would be altered. Any family member may suggest a goal for the family; the leader makes suggestions in the "how" procedures.

Several delivery systems have been devised for Alerian family counseling, but they have much in common with one another. Parental familiarity with the goals of children is important to all models. Of particular importance are the four goals of misbehavior which children use to find a place in the family. Often the goals are mistaken, and children do not gain the position in the family they most desire. These goals are (Dreikurs et al., 1974): 1) to gain attention; 2) to demonstrate power; 3) to punish or get even (retaliation); and 4) to demonstrate inadequacy.

To gain a position of strength in a family, a child will attempt many behaviors which have one of these four goals. The following are a few examples:

1. Throwing a tantrum in public to embarrass mother and dad shows your power as a child.

2. When as a five year old you demand help in dressing from other family members you are using inadequacy to gain what you want.

3. Two siblings start a fight near the telephone when mother is talking to someone to get attention focused on them and away from the phone conversation.

4. After having been disciplined a child starts a fight among other siblings which upsets what the parents are doing as a way of getting even (retaliation).

Learning the use of "natural consequences" as an alternative to powerful control of the child is another principle of Adlerian parent education. If parents can learn to allow children to experience the consequences of their acts, an honest and real learning situation is provided. Parents often do not allow this to occur because they feel the need to protect the child or to scold and/or punish instead (Dreikurs & Stoltz, 1964). Natural consequences do not need to be planned or structured but are a direct flow from the act as the following examples illustrate:

1.   If a child continuously gets up late and therefore misses the school bus, the natural consequence is walking to school and being late or, if it is a great distance, an unexcused absence from school.

2.   A child who refuses to eat his meals will eventually want a snack which is not there. All food is removed at the end of the meal and is not available again until the next scheduled meal.

Natural consequences allow parents to avoid a power struggle with a child by permitting the natural flow of events. It takes time to learn this skill and counselors will need to encourage parents frequently.

Parents also learn the use of logical consequences. Dreikurs and Grey (1968) define logical consequences as "situations where the consequence is, in effect, arranged by the parents or another adult rather than being solely the result of the child's own acts [p. 65]." An example is the case of a pre-schooler who wants to run into the street to play. Obviously a parent will not allow the natural consequence of a car hitting the child; however, one might make the child stay in the house or yard. The explanation would be made to the child that since he had gone into the street when asked not to do so, he will now have to stay inside.

Teaching parents to step back and avoid power struggles is another goal. This requires a great deal of interpretation and reinterpretation by the counselor. For many reasons, parents view avoiding power struggles as "letting the child get by" and feel "that makes me a weak parent." A counselor needs to spend considerable time helping parents see that by withdrawing their attention from the inappropriate behavior they are being stronger parents and will, in the end, be pleased to know that their children cannot draw them into a situation.

As all people—even children—are equal according to Adlerian philosophy, another goal of parent education is to gain their acceptance of *equality.* Children are equal in their rights, responsibilities and decisions. This does not mean children are the same. They are not as big; they are not as mature. We must not confuse equality with sameness. We do not own our children; as they grow, it becomes increasingly evident that they will and do make decisions, and accept or reject responsibilities. It is important therefore to respect children as people from an early age and to allow them equal rights.

A counselor who decides to try an Adlerian based parent education program will want to know how best to apply these principles. Below are several models one can follow.

## TRAINING PROCEDURES

### Mother Study Groups

This model was introduced by Dreikurs and has been used in many schools and agencies. A group of ten or so mothers meets once a week with a leader to learn new principles for living with children. Meetings can be held in members' homes, at school, or in any other designated location. They follow an outline or textbook which focuses on re-education of the parents and not on counseling or therapy. The groups are developmental in nature rather than crisis oriented. Parents are asked to read assignments between meetings. These, plus the experiences each parent is having, are discussed each week. While much is gained from the readings, the parents often gain their real insights through discussion with one another. When parents discover that theirs is not the only family in which mother pleads, begs and screams; father yells and sharply disciplines; and the children appear to be "in control" and getting their way, they begin to gain confidence in themselves and in the purposes of the group. As members begin to contribute their experiences, especially those which are examples of trying the new methods of responding to children, many parents will relax and start to experiment at home.

A Mother Study Group has a trained leader who lends support and assistance throughout the study. The leader can answer questions about the readings and give examples from daily living to demonstrate a point. Perhaps a more important role for the leader is encouraging mothers to try out the principles, taking specific problems and outlining a plan of action. An example would be assisting a mother to list all the chores around the house and make a "work chart" for family members. Another job for the leader is to point out to mothers how they play into their children's hands. For instance, mothers make rules such as all persons must pick up their own belongings; however, they become tired of the mess and pick everything up, thereby making the rule meaningless. Children learn from this experience that they can outlast mom and keep her their slave. In other words, the leader can begin to show mothers how they are in comparison to how they want to be. As group members become familiar with various patterns and traps they begin to share this role with the leader.

The members from the first Mother Study Group often become leaders of other groups, particularly if this is established as a goal for the first group, and time is spent on learning to be a leader. A Mother Study Group does not require highly skilled leaders. Part of its success builds on mothers helping each other, and the text can be used as a guideline for discussion.

Most Mother Study Groups use *Children: The Challenge,* written by Dreikurs and Stoltz (1964) as their text. Other possible references are:

1. *Raising a Responsible Child* by Dinkmeyer and McKay (1973).
2. *A Parent's Guide to Child Discipline* by Rudolph Dreikurs and Loren Grey (1970).
3. *Discipline without Tyranny* by Loren Grey (1972).
4. *Logical Consequences* by Rudolph Dreikurs and Loren Grey (1968).

### Father Study Groups

Another model of Adlerian parent education is Father Study Groups, which use the same format and text as Mother Study Groups. Some basic differences observed by the first author while using this model were:

1.   The atmosphere was less social and more businesslike. Fathers were cordial but less inclined to engage in general conversation.
2.   The leader was challenged more for evidence and proof of points being made.
3.   More time was needed for the giving up of physical control.
4.   A lot of discussion centered on the problem of fathers arranging for more time in their schedules for home and family life.

The fathers were positive about the opportunity to learn how to be better parents and pleased that someone at their child's school had included them in the group. The groups with fathers whose wives had also been through the material appeared to be more successful.

To provide groups for fathers, the counselor may need to work some evening hours. In addition, it is highly important for the counselor/leader to recognize the uneasiness fathers feel with this kind of exercise. Many are working with the old role assignments wherein children are the responsibility of the mother. The leader must be prepared for some serious challenges and must not be easily intimidated.

### Couple Study Groups

A third variation of the Study Group approach to Adlerian parent education has both parents attending at the same time. The first author used the same format and text as in the Mother Study Group. Five couples were invited for ten evening sessions in the counselor's office. At first members were reluctant to discuss any problems they were having with their children. However, as they completed their reading assignments they saw that their problems were common in families and they became more relaxed. Another hurdle for them was to describe a situation without blaming the other parent which was a rule laid down in the beginning. The group agreed to focus on developing more effective styles of relating to their children rather than trying to determine which parent was "wrong." It was interesting to note that a father from one family would listen very attentively to a mother from a second family describing a difficulty she was having, only to have his wife say at the end that she was having the same problem and he never would believe her when she tried to talk about it. In other words, they were often better able to see their own family's difficulties through another family's description. The greatest asset of this type of Study Group was that both parents could begin to change at the same time in deciding upon new rules, procedures and policies for their families. One parent did not have to go home to convince the other one to try some new things around the home. Parents could also encourage one another by pointing out improvements they saw at home. Group study helped parents begin to feel the sharing aspect of parenting; no longer did one parent feel burdened by the responsibility or alone in the job.

### Family Counseling Sessions

In this type of Adlerian parent education, all members of a family meet with the counselor at a school, guidance center, church or other facility. Generally the counselor has all members begin by describing a typical day at their house. Who gets up first? Who starts breakfast? Who leaves the house first? What other morning chores or responsibilities are there? What grade is each of the children in? How does each do in school? Who comes home first? What responsibilities are there at dinner time? Usually the mother or father starts the description with other members adding thoughts and opinions as the description progresses. Often the parent will say something like "Johnny doesn't get up when he is called." Johnny will then agree or disagree.

After twenty minutes or so of this the counselor interviews the children separately from their parents, asking questions such as "Who starts fights at your house?" or "Who doesn't do their chores?" Many questions focus around how the children see themselves in relation to the family group. Feelings of inadequacy, loss of power and being picked on appear during the discussion. Next the counselor interviews the parents alone to hear them describe how they see things at home. Often parents feel one child is causing them the most concern. Parents are concerned over a child doing poorly at school, one who doesn't do anything he/she is asked, one who seems too quiet and alone. The counselor gives them several suggestions to see how they might work at their house. The parents' response gives the counselor some feeling for how flexible the parents are and what they might feel comfortable trying.

Finally, all family members are called together again. The counselor presents or discusses what he/she sees as some of the problems they should be working on, explaining how he/she heard these things from the children's and parents' descriptions. An example might be that mother has complained the children do not come home in time for dinner, arriving late and wanting to eat. A new approach would be that mother gives notice to all members as to the time of dinner, serves dinner to whomever is at home, and clears the table when they finish. Late arrivers can either go without dinner or fix it themselves as well as clean up all dishes and pans. Another example might be the toys, books, and clothing left around the house, which mother unsuccessfully has asked to be picked up, and which she eventually picks up herself. A new approach might be that anything mother picks up becomes her property to sell back or throw away. Another session may lead to discussion of what the family members are doing about fighting with each other, distribution of work chores, getting parents' attention and so forth. All members participate in planning for the next week so there are no agendas hidden from the children. The counselor introduces the family to the principles of respect for each other and equality of all members. Thus, the sessions are both counseling and educational in nature.

Originally these sessions were a part of Dreikurs' child guidance center programs. He and his staff noticed so much in common from family to family that they decided to demonstrate family counseling sessions in front of an audience (Dreikurs et al., 1959). As parents watch the demonstration family, they learn about patterns of interaction and the results these have in family relationships. The demonstration family has the same everyday problems as other families, so others identify with them and learn from the counseling session as well. In situations when counselors do not have enough time for all the people they serve, this method provides services to more people. In addition, many families are too shy or embarrassed to actually come to a counselor about their family relationships but sincerely want to do a better job at home. These families can learn a great deal from a demonstration family counseling session. As these techniques become known, and therefore trusted, more families are willing to volunteer as demonstration families. Counselors will find that participating families recommend these sessions to their neighbors, friends and relatives.

### Family Councils or Family Meetings

Family Councils are defined in the subtitle of Dreikurs' new book on the subject, *Family Council: The Dreikurs Technique for Putting an End to War between Parents and Children (and between Children and Children)* (Dreikurs, Gould, & Corsini, 1974). As noted earlier in this chapter, our society is moving from authoritarian relationships toward democratic relationships. As parents try to keep harmony in the home, they find they do not know how to bring democratic living to their full and busy lives. The Family Council approach is designed for parents striving toward democratic living, with respect for all members of the family and acceptance of equality for each member. Dreikurs, et al. (1974) base their promotion of Family Councils on the following propositions:

1. *The Family is an Organization.* It should operate in an orderly manner, each member knowing what to do and what acceptable limits are.

2. *Emotions Follow Intellect and Behavior.* We like and are kindest to those who treat us nicely. This calls for family members to find ways to be more cooperative with one another.

3. *Human Beings Can Function Only as Equals.* Respect and equality must be present, not only from child toward parent, but also from parent to child and child to child, to allow all members to do their best.

4. *Logic Works Better Than Force.* Parents must avoid the use of bribes, threats or pleading with the child to gain better family relationships.

5. *Human Relationships are Logical.* Parents should allow their children to experience the consequences of their acts early in life, as the world will function this way when they are grown.

6. *Parents and Children are Engaged in a Cooperative Venture.* All family members have a responsibility for the family. Therefore, they must know that their contributions to the family are respected. Parents do not have sole responsibility for the family.

7. *Well-Being Depends on Cooperation.* Children must learn cooperation rather than selfishness, self-centeredness and unhappiness.

Dreikurs, et al. define a Family Council as:

> A group of people who live together, whether or not they are related by blood or marriage. The group shall have regularly scheduled meetings and operate under rules agreed upon in advance. The meetings shall be an open forum at which all family members can speak without interruption, with freedom of expression, without fear of consequences, and without regard for age or status. Its deliberations result in decision only when all members present agree—that is, come to a common understanding [p. 7].

In organizing a Family Council some simple steps need to be taken such as setting a date and time, making sure all family members are invited, establishing rules and agenda. Sessions are not held for members to complain about all the little things upsetting them, but rather as a technique for building better communications and resolving conflicts. It takes families several weeks of meeting before they feel comfortable with this method, and they may need encouragement from a counselor to continue. A counselor can also point out where communications have failed on account of their not respecting each other's views or not allowing all members to participate to their fullest. Families need time to decide whether this method works better than screaming, yelling and fighting.

### "C" Groups

Dinkmeyer designed this technique after years of work with parents and counselors (Dinkmeyer & Arciniega, 1972; and Dinkmeyer, 1973c). The "C" group helps parents understand children's behavior and their own reactions to that behavior. "C" groups differ from discussion or study groups in that they consider how parents' feelings hamper their ability to relate successfully to their children. As educators stress the need to work with the "whole child," counselors using this technique work with the "whole parent." "C" groups consider the affective, cognitive and behavioral domains of the parent. The name "C group" derives from seven basic components beginning with the letter "c":

1. *Collaboration.* All members of the group are equal, including the leader.
2. *Consultation.* Parents and leader help and advise each other.

3. *Clarification.* Group members help each other clarify what goes on and how beliefs hamper efforts.
4. *Confrontation* provides honest feedback to the group.
5. *Concern* of the group for each member.
6. *Confidentiality.* The group treats all discussion as confidential.
7. *Commitment.* Parents commit themselves to change themselves and the patterns of communication at home, rather than dedicating their efforts to changing the children.

At the first session each parent introduces himself or herself and briefly describes some specific concerns with one of the children. When introductions are complete, the leader spends a small amount of time on general principles. However, Dinkmeyer warns the counselor not to allow this to remove the focus from specific concerns with children! The leader asks one parent to present a specific occurrence at home and to describe his or her feelings when the child behaved this way. The counselor then guides the group in looking at what might be the purpose of the behavior and possible alternatives. It is a good idea to end the meeting by reviewing with each parent what he or she is going to do differently during the next week. These plans provide the starting point for the next meeting. All parents should be at every meeting! If one or two parents dominate, attendance will begin to drop.

## TRAINING OF TRAINERS

Training of leaders in Adlerian family counseling can be a part of a Master's program in guidance and counseling, social work or school psychology. Currently, however, most training is through demonstrations, workshops and postgraduate seminars. In addition, many receive training through courses at such places as the Alfred Adler Institute in Chicago.

Training revolves around coursework in Adlerian philosophy and theory, procedures in family counseling and practicums in family counseling. Dinkmeyer suggests that training of leaders for "C" groups be attempted only after the counselor has developed competencies in group process and communication (Dinkmeyer, 1973c). Inherent in this training approach is belief in the principles listed as important for parents. In addition to applying these principles to family counseling, training applies them to individual and group counseling. Trainers for Mother Study Groups may be para-professionals when school counselors or others train mothers to lead these groups.

## RESOURCES

Alfred Adler Institute, 110 South Dearborn Street, Chicago, Illinois 60603.

American Society of Adlerian Psychology, 110 South Dearborn Street, Suite 1400, Chicago, Illinois 60603.

Parent Education Association, P. O. Box 18, Columbia, Missouri.

## REFERENCES

Berrett, R.D., & Kelley, R. Discipline and the hearing impaired child. *Volta Review,* 1975, **77**, 117–124.

Christensen, O. C. Education: A model for counseling in the elementary school. *Elementary School Guidance and Counseling Journal,* 1969, **4**, 12–19.

Christensen, O. C. Family Education: A model for consultation. *Elementary School Guidance and Counseling Journal,* 1972, **1**, 121–9.

Christensen, O. C. & Haak, M. A. *A guide to parents.* Tucson: Tucson Public Schools and Department of Counseling, University of Arizona, 1969.

Dinkmeyer, D. Elementary school guidance: Principles and functions. *The School Counselor,* 1968, **16**, 11–16. (a)

Dinkmeyer, D. *Guidance and counseling in the elementary school.* New York: Holt, Rinehart and Winston, Inc., 1968. (b)

Dinkmeyer, D. Consulting: A strategy for change. *The School Counselor,* 1973, 52–55. (a)

Dinkmeyer, D. Elementary school counseling: Prospects and potentials. *Personnel and Guidance Journal,* 1973, **52**, 171–174. (b)

Dinkmeyer, D. The parent "C" group. *Personnel and Guidance Journal,* 1973, **52**, 252–256. (c)

Dinkmeyer, D. & Arciniega, M. Affecting the learning climate through "C" groups with teachers. *The School Counselor,* 1972, Vol 19 No. 4 249–253.

Dinkmeyer, D. & Dreikurs, R. *Encouraging children to learn: The encouragement process.* Englewood Cliffs, N.J.: Prentice-Hall, 1963.

Dinkmeyer, D. & McKay, G. D. Leading effective parent study groups. *Elementary School Guidance and Counseling Journal,* 1974, **9**, 108–115.

Dinkmeyer, D. & McKay, G. D. *Raising a responsible child: Practical steps to successful family relationships.* New York: Simon and Schuster, 1973.

Dreikurs, R. *The challenge of parenthood.* New York: Drell, Sloan and Pearce, 1948.

Dreikurs, R., Corsini, R., Lowe, R., & Sonstegard, M. *Adlerian family counseling—a manual for counseling centers.* Eugene, Ore.: University of Oregon Press, 1959.

Dreikurs, R., Gould, S. & Corsini, R. *Family council.* Chicago: Henry Regnery Co., 1974.

Dreikurs, R., & Grey, L. *Logical consequences.* New York: Meredith Press, 1968.

Dreikurs, R., & Grey, L. *A parent's guide to child discipline.* New York: Hawthorn Books, Inc., 1970.

Dreikurs, R., & Stoltz, V. *Children and challenge.* New York: Hawthorn Books, Inc., 1964.

Frazier, F., & Matthes, W. A. Parent education: A comparision of Adlerian and behavioral approaches. *Elementary School Guidance and Counseling,* 1975, **10**, 31–38.

Grey, L. *Discipline without tyranny (child training during the first five years).* New York: Hawthorn Books, Inc., 1972.

Gushurst, R. S. The technique, utility, and validity of life style analysis. *Counseling Psychologist,* 1971, **3**, 30–40.

Lamb, J., & Deschenes, R. The unique role of the elementary school counselor. *Elementary School Guidance & Counseling Journal,* 1973, **8**, 219–223.

Lowe, R. N., & Christensen, O. E. *Guide to enrollees.* Eugene, Ore.: University of Oregon Press, 1966.

Piercy, F. P. *Broadening the scope of elementary school counseling: Some Adlerian strategies.* Gainesville: University of Florida Press, 1972.

*Proceedings of a symposium on family counseling and therapy.* Athens, Ga.: University of Georgia Press, 1971.

Salty, N. *Study group leader's manual.* Chicago: Alfred Adler Institute, 1967.

Tindall, J. Middle/junior high school counselor's corner. *Elementary School Guidance & Counseling Journal,* 1974, **9**, 159 164.

VanHoose, W., Peitrofesa, J. J., & Carlson, J. *Elementary school guidance and counseling: A composite view.* Boston: Houghton-Mifflin, 1973.

Watson, R. I. *The great psychologists: Aristotle to Freud.* Philadelphia: I. B. Lippincott Co., 1963.

This model of parent education is based on the principles of Rogerian counseling. Expression and recognition of feelings by all family members, development of insight and understanding by each family member, and learning how to listen are basic concepts of this model. Parent Effectiveness Training is described in this chapter as an example of client-centered parent education.

*Chapter 3*

# CLIENT-CENTERED PARENT EDUCATION

## HISTORY

This model of parent education owes its beginnings to Carl Rogers, who brought counseling to a higher level of development. Prior to his influence on the profession, counselors operated within two basic frameworks: vocational counseling (as promoted by Frank Parsons) and the psychoanalytic model prominent in social work and psychology. Basically, Rogers designed a role where the counselor remained "nondirective" with clients. The method became popularly known as client centered counseling or therapy. During the 1950's and 1960's this approach became the dominant one for training school counselors. School counseling programs today are still dominated by Rogerian oriented counselors.

## BASIC ASSUMPTIONS

Underlying this client oriented approach to counseling is a philosophy that man is basically good and will, if allowed to do so, do the right or best thing. Also, one must believe that humans are always capable of making their own choices and decisions and only need support during a time of difficulty or indecision. Another assumption is that the client is responsible for his or her own decisions and, therefore, the counselor or therapist does not take responsibility for structuring their work together. Inherent in this approach is the belief that each individual has the capacity for constructive self-change.

## GOALS

Important to any discussion of the goals of client centered parent education programs is the recognition that the client/parent comes for help of his or her volition. Therapy begins with a person in a state of stress who chooses to seek assistance. Generally accepted goals representative of client-centered counseling with an individual or group follow:

1. *Free expression of feelings.* By maintaining a permissive and accepting attitude, the counselor encourages client self-awareness and expression of feelings.
2. *Recognition of feelings and assumptions.* The client sees feelings and assumptions as what they are and no longer hides them (even from him/herself). At first there is recognition of negative feelings, and gradually positive feelings emerge.
3. *Insight and understanding.* These develop as feelings are released and clarified. Elements of the client's insight are:

a.  experiencing, understanding, and accepting aspects of him/herself previously repressed;

b.  more clearly understanding the causes of his/her behavior and accepting these experiences in his/her life;

c.  clarifying possible courses of positive action.

4.  *Taking positive steps.* As time passes and insight develops, possible positive alternatives present themselves. The client then begins the process of selecting a course of action. Again, it is the function of the counselor only to recognize and clarify and not to lead the client.

5.  *Ending the contact.* The decision to terminate is made by the client.

These goals also apply to client centered parent education programs. In summary the effects of client centered work with families, are according to Rogers (1970):

1.  More expression of feelings to members of the family, both negative and positive.

2.  Discovery that expressing true feelings is a deeply satisfying experience.

3.  As expressions of feelings progress, these feelings lose their explosiveness. This allows family members to express feelings more positively.

4.  Realization that a relationship can be lived on the basis of real feelings, rather than on the basis of defensive pretense, even though there is a fluctuating variety of feelings which exist.

5.  Learning to initiate and maintain two way communication. To be understood and to understand others is where it all begins.

6.  Movement toward permitting each member of the family to have his or her own feelings and be a person. This develops as each person discovers he or she can trust

his/her own feelings and reactions and trust and accept others' feelings.

Rogers sees members of family circles becoming separate and unique persons, with individual goals and values, bound together by real feelings. The responsibility for direction is placed upon the client; the counselor must tell parents in the beginning that he/she will not have all the answers. Also the pace of the program is set by the client, which means that he/she is not pushed.

Moustakas and Makowsky (1952) point out that the client centered approach works best with clients who see the problem as focused in themselves and who are willing to accept responsibility for their own difficulties. They say this approach is not widely accepted by parents for the following reasons:

1.   Parents see the problem as the child's, not theirs.
2.   They come seeking the "right way."
3.   They come as a last resort and demand definite answers.
4.   Counselor reflection of their feelings is inadequate.

Therefore Moustakas and Makowsky call for a program with the following format:

1.   Reflect and clarify when appropriate.
2.   Present child development information in answer to direct questions, leaving evaluation of information to parents.
3.   Answer questions with a tentative explanation or description of the child's progress.
4.   Give support to parents.
5.   Avoid being educative (i.e., be tentative rather than authoritative).

Occasional articles in counseling journals show how counselors attempt to adapt client centered counseling principles to efforts in parent education (McWhirter & Kahn, 1974; Penn & Bolding, 1974; Sauber, 1971). However, the model which seems to have had the greatest impact on the school counselor is Parent Effectiveness Training (P.E.T.), devised by Thomas Gordon. We have chosen this model to demonstrate a client centered parent education program.

## TRAINING PROCEDURES

### Parent Effectiveness Training

This program of parent education is billed as "the 'no-lose' program for raising responsible children." Gordon (1970) started working in parent education when he became aware that "parents are blamed and not trained [p.1]." Initially he started a course for parents who were already having problems with their children. It readily became apparent that this technique could be used by almost any parents who so desired.

Underlying P.E.T. is the belief that parents and children can live together with warmth, based on mutual love and respect. Gordon points out that for some reason when people become parents they forget they are people. They start acting as they think parents should behave. Unfortunately they form the image of good parents by watching friends, listening to relatives, and remembering how they were raised. Comments such as, "When I was young my mother always did this and I turned out okay," seem to give credibility to what parents do with their own children. Also, as parents, people are and will continue to be inconsistent unless they are able to learn new ways of communicating with their children. P.E.T. program leaders believe that nonprofessionals can learn the skills used by professionals in helping their children and in communicating with them. In fact Gordon points out that for far too many years the professionals have communicated solely with one another when they should have been communicating with others outside the profession, such as parents.

P.E.T. has been described as a complete system of parent education. It is built on these premises:

1.  Training before trouble occurs in a family, aiming primarily at young parents or couples without children as yet.

2.  Punishment can be discarded forever.

3.  Teenagers do not rebel against parents, they rebel against certain destructive methods of discipline.

4.  Parents can and will be inconsistent because their feelings change from day to day, from child to child; to be consistent would mean being "false."

5.  Parents don't have to put up a united front, for to do so denies each person's true feelings.

6.  Active listening is the key to good relations between parents and kids.

7.  Parents are stuck with I win-you lose or You win-I lose approaches.

Gordon describes or defines parents by separating them into three distinct groups. They are:

1.  *The Winners,* who:
    a.  strongly defend their use of power and the exercise of authority over their children;
    b.  believe in restricting, setting limits, demanding certain behaviors, giving commands, demanding obedience;
    c.  when conflicts arise, *win and the child loses;*
    d.  may be recognized by counselors through such remarks as, "It is the responsibility of

the parent to use authority," or, "Parents know best," and, "It's for the child's own good."

2. *The Losers,* who:
   a. allow their children a great deal of freedom;
   b. avoid setting limits;
   c. are proud of the fact that they are not authoritarian;
   d. when conflicts arise, *lose and the child wins.*

3. *The Oscillators,* who:
   a. find it impossible to follow one approach;
   b. swing back and forth between strict and lenient, tough and easy;
   c. when conflicts arise, *sometimes win and sometimes lose;*
   d. are the most confused parents and whose children are often the most disturbed.

Parents frequently see only two alternatives for conflicts: "You win-I lose" and "You lose-I win." P.E.T. is a no-lose approach to settling conflicts.

This no-lose approach builds on several techniques. The first skill is "active listening," a method of encouraging children to accept responsibility for finding solutions to their own problems. Parents must come to know and recognize their own feelings first and then their children's. All parents have areas of acceptance and areas of nonacceptance. Gordon uses a rectangle to represent schematically all possible behaviors of children. Parents are asked to divide a rectangle to show their levels of acceptance and nonacceptance.

| Area of Acceptance |
|:---:|
| Area of Nonacceptance |

A rectangle for "accepting" parents would look like this:

| Acceptance |
| --- |
| Nonacceptance |

One for "nonaccepting" parents would look like this:

| Acceptance |
| --- |
| Nonacceptance |

Rectangles for all parents vary with each of their children and according to what the conflict is over. Gordon feels these graphic presentations help parents see their feelings and the conditions that cause feelings to change. To be an effective parent one must recognize one's humanness, and recognize negative and positive feelings toward one's children. This is one part of active listening. Too frequently parents believe that nonacceptance is more helpful to their children than acceptance; therefore they rely on evaluation, judgment, criticism, admonishing and commanding. They believe they must tell a child what they don't accept about him or her before he or she can be better.

In P.E.T. parents learn to communicate acceptance both nonverbally and verbally. They learn they can show acceptance by:

1.   Not intervening in the child's activities and allowing him or her freedom.
2.   Learning to say nothing—just listening.
3.   Learning the "Typical Twelve" categories of parents' verbal responses.

These Typical Twelve responses are (Gordon, 1970):

   1.   Ordering, Directing, Commanding
        Telling the child to do something, giving an order or
        a command.

2.  Warning, Admonishing, Threatening
    Telling the child what consequences will occur if he
    or she does something.
3.  Exhorting, Moralizing, Preaching
    Telling the child what he/she should or ought to do.
4.  Advising, Giving Solutions or Suggestions
    Telling the child how to solve a problem, giving
    advice or suggestions; providing answers or solu-
    tions.
5.  Lecturing, Teaching, Giving Logical Arguments
    Trying to influence the child with facts, counterargu-
    ments, logic, information, or your own opinions.
6.  Judging, Criticizing, Disagreeing, Blaming
    Making a negative judgment or evaluation of the
    child.
7.  Praising, Agreeing
    Offering a positive evaluation or judgment; agree-
    ing.
8.  Name Calling, Ridiculing, Shaming
    Making the child feel foolish; putting the child into
    a category; shaming.
9.  Interpreting, Analyzing, Diagnosing
    Telling the child what his/her motives are or analyz-
    ing why he/she is doing or saying something; com-
    municating that you have him/her figured out or
    diagnosed.
10. Reassuring, Sympathizing, Counseling, Supporting
    Trying to make the child feel better; talking him or
    her out of feelings; trying to make feelings go away;
    denying the strength of his/her feelings.
11. Probing, Questioning, Interrogating
    Trying to find reasons, motives, causes; searching
    for more information to help you solve the problem.
12. Withdrawing, Distracting, Humoring, Diverting
    Trying to get the child away from the problem; with-
    drawing from the problem yourself; distracting the
    child, kidding, pushing the problem aside [pp. 41–
    44].

Ninety per cent of parents' responses fall into one of
these categories. They need to learn that none of these
responses brings to the relationship the kind of communi-

cation they desire. Most, if not all of these, shut the door on communication. P.E.T. helps parents learn new responses to reopen the door.

Once this door between parent and child is open, parents must learn "door openers" to keep communication moving. Some of these are: "Oh," "I see," "Really," "No kidding," "Tell me about it," "Let's discuss it," "This seems important to you."

In active listening the receiver tries actively to *understand* what the sender is feeling and what his/her message *means*. The receiver does not send a message of his/her own but rather feeds back only what he/she feels the sender's message meant. Active listening will:

1.  Help children find out what they really are feeling.
2.  Help children become less afraid of negative feelings.
3.  Promote a relationship of warmth between parent and child.
4.  Facilitate problem solving by the child because he/she can talk it out.
5.  Keep the ball in the child's ball park.

Basic attitudes a parent must demonstrate before mastery of active listening are as follows (Gordon, 1970):

1.  A parent must want to hear what the child has to say.
2.  A parent must genuinely want to be helpful to the child with the particular problem at that time.
3.  A parent must genuinely be able to accept his or her feelings.
4.  A parent must have a deep feeling of trust in the child's capacity to handle feelings, to work through them, and to find solutions to problems.
5.  A parent must feel that feelings are transitory, not permanent.

6.   A parent must be able to see the child as someone separate from him or herself [pp.59–60].

Before putting these new skills to work, parents must be aware of problem ownership. Sometimes the child owns the problem, and in this case active listening is a good idea. When a parent owns the problem he or she becomes a sender. This chart is helpful for counselors to use with parents:

| *When the child owns the problem* | *When the parent owns the problem* |
|---|---|
| Child initiates communication | Parent initiates communication |
| Parent is a listener | Parent is a sender |
| Parent is a counselor | Parent is an influencer |
| Parent wants to help child | Parent wants to help him or herself |
| Parent is a "sounding board" | Parent wants to "sound off" |
| Parent helps child find a solution | Parent has to find his or her own solution |
| Parent accepts child's solution | Parent must be satisfied with solution him/herself |
| Parent is primarily interested in child's needs | Parent is primarily interested in own needs |
| Parent is more passive | Parent is more aggressive |

(Gordon, 1970, p. 107).

When parents own the problem they have three alternatives: trying to modify the child directly, modifying the environment, and modifying themselves. Too often when attempting to modify the child, parents send solutions or put-down messages to the child. Counselors must bring parents to a point where they learn the differences between sending "you-messages" and "I-messages." I-messages are expressions of how a situation is making a parent feel. They are more acceptable to children and once again place responsibility with them. You-messages are evaluative and critical and increase the conflict. Examples are:

| You Messages | I Messages |
|---|---|
| You'd better stop that | I cannot read when someone is hitting me |
| You are bad | I don't feel like playing when I have a cold |
| You are being silly | I sure get sad when I see the room dirty again |
| Don't you ever... | |

Many parent-child conflicts are not solved by confrontation or changes in the environment. When these conflicts occur most parents think once again in win-lose terms. Gordon identifies Method I (parents win) of conflict resolution as the time when parents:

1. Select a solution.
2. Announce it and hope the child will accept it.
3. First use persuasion to influence the child, later use power and authority.

Problems with Method I are:

1. Low motivation for the child to carry out the solution.
2. Resentment toward parents.
3. Difficulties in enforcement.
4. Lack of opportunity for the child to develop self-discipline.

Method II, in which the children supposedly win, is characterized by children who:

1. Learn how to throw temper tantrums to control parents.

2.  Make parents feel guilty.
3.  Say nasty, deprecating things to their parents.
4.  Are wild and unmanageable.
5.  Believe their needs are the most important.
6.  Lack inner controls on their behavior and become very self-centered.
7.  Have peer difficulties.
8.  Have difficulty adjusting to school.
9.  Develop feelings of insecurity about their parents' love.

Method III is the no-lose method for resolving conflicts. This method is for those who view each other as equals, having relatively equal power. This is a system in which everyone wins, as the solution must be acceptable to all. Briefly, here is how it works. Parent and child encounter a conflict of needs situation. They agree to work together toward a solution acceptable to both. One or both offer solutions which are possible. After critical evaluation by those involved, a decision is reached. No selling or power moves are necessary because both parties have agreed to the solution. Gordon (1970) defines Method III as follows: "Method III, then, is a method by which each unique parent and his unique child can solve each of their unique conflicts by finding their own unique solutions acceptable to both [p. 200]."

Why is this effective? Probably because everyone participates and makes a commitment to a solution. It eliminates the need for power and requires less enforcement. A big plus is that family members are able to locate the real problem.

The P.E.T. trainer's task is to help parents develop the use of Method III. The six steps to Method III are as follows:

1.  Identify and define the conflict.
2.  Generate possible alternative solutions.

3. Evaluate the alternative solutions.
4. Decide on the best acceptable solution.
5. Work out ways of implementing the solution.
6. Follow up to evaluate how it worked.

Parents typically encounter problems of:

1. Initial distrust and resistance.
2. Not finding an acceptable solution.
3. Reverting to Method I.
4. Building punishment into the decision.
5. Broken agreements.

One last lesson supplied by P.E.T. is how to avoid being fired as a parent. Parents get fired by their kids when they hassle and harangue them to change beliefs and values. Adolescents do not want to be denied their basic civil rights. On the other hand, parents ask, "Can't I teach my values?" In answer, Gordon suggests that a "do as I do" approach is advisable and not the "do as I say, not as I do" approach. Parents can learn to be consultants to their children–sharing, offering, and suggesting, but not preaching or imposing. A simple recommended exercise is to take a piece of paper and divide it into two parts labeled, "Problems Agreed to be Child's Responsibility" and "Problems That Must be Problem Solved," and to list areas of difficulty in the appropriate category. Those in the first section need no mutual problem solving as they belong to the child. Those in the second will require mutual problem solving. This may help when children have decided not to trust their parents or any new methods. The children are so happy to have all the items in the left column gone from the "hassle" that they gladly cooperate on those in the right column.

When parents decide to modify the environment they can do so by enriching, impoverishing, simplifying or childproofing it; limiting the child's life space; or substituting one activity for another. Counselors should be sure parents know how to prepare their children for changes in the environment before any changes take place. It is especially important to plan ahead with older children, making sure they feel included.

Modifying themselves as parents is probably the part of problem solving most threatening to parents and most difficult to accept. It is much easier to concentrate on changing children or the environment. A counselor must bring a parent to ask the question, "How much do I like who I am?" Many parents have difficulty ridding themselves of the value system under which they were raised that now causes problems for them with their children. Others have a feeling of ownership of their children. Still others want to make their children fit a mold. Key questions to use with parents are:

1.   Can you become more accepting of yourself?
2.   Whose children are they?
3.   Do you really like children or just a certain type of child?
4.   Are your values and beliefs the only true ones?
5.   Is your primary relationship with your spouse?

Many parents, once they begin to learn to express and accept true feelings, grow to accept much more flexibility in their relationships with their children. Lillibridge's study (1972) shows that parents who participated in the P.E.T. program improved significantly in their overall attitudes towards their children. Parents' confidence in themselves as parents and acceptance of their children showed significant improvement. Stearn (1971) finds that P.E.T. trained parents become more democratic in their attitudes toward the family. Therefore, it is possible for counselors to work toward a goal of having parents modify themselves.

## RESOURCES

P.E.T. Information. Effectiveness Training Associates, 110 South Euclid Avenue, Pasadena, California 91101.

## REFERENCES

Benson, L., Berger, M., & Mease, W. Family communication systems. *Small Group Behavior,* 1975, **6,** 91–105.

Gordon, T. *Parent effectiveness training: The "no-lose" program for raising responsible children.* New York: Peter H. Wyden, 1970.

Gordon, T. *On being an effective parent.* Washington, D.C.: American Personnel and Guidance Association, 1607 New Hampshire Avenue, N.W., Washington, D.C. 20009, 1973 (Film).

Guerney, B. Filial therapy: Description and rationale. *Journal of Consulting Psychology,* 1964, **28,** 304–310.

Guerney, B., Stover, L., & Andronico, M. P. On educating disadvantaged parents to motivate children for learning: A filial approach. *Community Mental Health Journal,* 1967, **3**(1), 66–72.

Howard, D. The professional parent. *Journal of Emotional Education,* 1969, **9**(3), 96–101.

Kallman, J. R., & Stollak, G. E. *Maternal behavior toward children in need arousing situations.* Paper presented at the Midwestern Psychological Association, Chicago, Illinois, 1974.

Kamali, M. R. A study of the effectiveness of counseling in a community parent-teacher education center (Doctoral dissertation, University of Oregon, 1967). *Dissertation Abstracts International,* 1968, **29,** 123A–124A, (University Microfilms No. 68–10,000).

Larson, R. Can parent classes affect family communications? *School Counselor,* 1972, **19,** 261–270.

Lillibridge, E. M. The relationship of a Parent Effectiveness Training program to change in parents self-assured attitudes and children's perceptions of parents (Doctoral dissertation, United States International University, 1972). *Dissertation Abstracts International,* 1972, **32,** 5613A.

McWhirter, J. J., & Kahn, S. E. A parent education group. *Elementary School Guidance and Counseling Journal,* 1974, **9,** 116–122.

Moustakas, C. E., & Makowsky, G. Client-centered therapy with parents. *Journal of Consulting Psychologists,* 1952, **16,** 338–342.

Penn, L., & Bolding, J. Helping talks for helping children. *Elementary School Guidance and Counseling Journal,* 1974, **9,** 132–137.

Rogers, C. R. *On becoming a person.* Boston: Houghton-Mifflin, 1970.

Sauber, S. R. Multiple-family group counseling. *Personnel and Guidance Journal,* 1971, **49,** 459–465.

Slavson, S. R. *Child-centered group guidance of parents.* New York: International Universities Press, 1958.

Stearn, M. B. The relationship of parent effectiveness training to parent attitudes, parent behavior and child self-esteem (Doctoral dissertation, United States International University, 1971). *Dissertation Abstracts International,* 1971, **32,** 1885A–1886A.

The behavioral model of parent education assumes that much of the behavior of both parents and children is learned. If a behavior is learned, it is subject to change by relearning. The task of the parent educator and subsequently the parent is to look for the types of environmental changes that will result in new learning on the part of the child. In a sense, this model trains parents as behavioral technicians or environmental engineers. As such they learn observational skills, behavior influence procedures, and means of evaluating their own performance.

*Chapter 4*

# BEHAVIORAL PARENT EDUCATION

## History

The model of parent training currently receiving most recognition in professional literature is based on behavior modification approaches. In terms of their applications to direct work with parents these approaches have been developing since the late 1950's. There have been a number of attempts to define behavior modification, with the general consensus involving some type of intervention based on techniques derived from learning theory. Most writers feel that to qualify as behavior modification, an intervention needs to involve some systematic use of these techniques. Breger and McGaugh (1965) wrote a critique of behavioral approaches and took the position that such a definition of behavior modification was, if not erroneous, at least misleading. Their contention was that no theory of learning was fully accepted and that many techniques of behavior modification had little if any relationship to laboratory studies of human or animal learning.

Regardless of criticisms, behavioral techniques have flourished. A more recent article by London (1972) takes a practical approach to behavior modification, suggesting that practitioners look for empirically proven techniques and apply them because they work and not because of learning theory. In general, parent training using behavioral techniques takes a middle ground position by using principles primarily derived from operant conditioning, social learning theory, and the experimental analysis of behavior; applying them; and seeing if they work. If they are demonstrated to be effective, they are applied to new cases and settings.

The majority of the early references on behavioral parent training involved training parents as therapists for their own children (Guerney, 1969; Hawkins, Peterson, Schweid, & Bijou, 1966; Hirsch & Walder, 1968; Johnson & Brown, 1969, Mathis, 1971; Shah, 1969; Wagner, 1968; Wahler, Winkel, Peterson, & Morrison, 1965; Wetzel, Baker, Roney & Martin, 1966; Zeilberger, Sampen, & Sloane, 1968). Several excellent review articles trace the development, range of use, techniques, and outcomes of early attempts at training parents (Cone & Sloop, 1974; Berkowitz & Graziano, 1972; Johnson & Katz, 1973; O'Dell, 1974; Tavormina, 1974).

Of historical note is the group parent training first reported by Pumroy (1965). Prior to this effort and in a majority of subsequent approaches one family received training at a time. The first families trained under the behavioral model were those who came to a mental health facility because of children's behavior. Hence the tradition of single family training. Since the problems were usually rather severe, the children were identified as exceptional

children. Also because of the degree of behavior disturbance, the parents did not feel capable of adequately managing the behavior and were prime candidates for any type
of parent education program. Many of the earliest references were written in university connected facilities, where
the management of behavior of disturbed children by
means of behavioral techniques was beginning to receive
considerable attention. The inclusion of parents in these
behavioral programs so that programs could continue at
home was the next logical step. The focus on training parents of exceptional children to become part, if not the
major source, of direct intervention with their children has
been reported for the following child behaviors or problems: autism, retardation, enuresis, self-injurious behavior,
school phobia, delinquency, speech problems including
stuttering and elective mutism, encopresis, hyperactivity,
problems associated with brain damage, antisocial responses, immaturity, aggressive responses, psychotic behavior, tantrums and withdrawal. Even though these early
reports of behavioral parent training involved exceptional
children, many of the children's problems may be seen as
developmental. Many children exhibit one or more of these
problems at some point in their development without being referred to a mental health facility for treatment. Accordingly, once it was demonstrated that parents could be
taught to manage severe behavior problems, trainers began
working with parents on more common concerns.

## BASIC ASSUMPTIONS

The basic assumption behind behavior modification approaches to training parents (or anyone, for that matter) is
that a great deal of human behavior results from learning.
It follows, then, that if a behavior is learned, it is subject to
such learning issues as forgetting and relearning. Accord-

ingly, if learning is the basic *problem,* then learning must be the basic *solution.* Another basic assumption is that much learning results from the interaction of the individual with the environment. The conclusion that follows is that the environment must change prior to any change in behavior that originally related to the environment. Emphasis on environmental influences on learning and the social settings of learning clearly sets the stage for using the behavioral model in parent training.

## GOALS

One of the goals most represented in the training of parents within a behavioral model relates directly to the type of diagnostic evaluation or assessment. This general evaluation scheme comprises the determination of the existence of three types of problems: 1) Does the person do too much of something? 2) Does the person do too little of something? 3) Is there a problem with the person not continuing to do something that is valued or seen as appropriate? These are referred to as problems of excesses, deficits, and maintenance respectively. Parental behaviors or parenting skills are amenable to this same type of assessment.

It is clear that the very terms excesses, deficits, and maintenance problems imply social value judgments. Many critics of behavior modification take the position that such value judgments must be removed from the helping professions. However, proponents of the behavioral approach hold that such judgments are made within the typical course of human interactions and that making such judgments more openly meets ethical concerns. The authors of this publication take the position that value judgments are being made at all times when the concept of training is involved. Training for or in what? Anytime you train someone, you have taken the position that it would be "better" for the person to have this new skill or concept. "Better" is obviously a value judgment.

The training of parents using the behavioral model focuses on increasing parental skills in influencing, controlling and directing behavior and development, so that parents act as agents of change for their children. Parents have clearly indicated that they desire practical skills in child management (Moustakas & Makowsky, 1952). The selection of areas where the children are to be changed fits the assessment scheme of deficits, excesses and problems of maintenance outlined above. The basic goal of behavioral parent training is to have the parents, who are the most significant part in the child's environment, accept the responsibility for changing their own child. This in turn assumes that the parent will change by acquiring more skills. These increased skills could take the form of remediating parental deficits or excesses or keeping the parent engaged in a certain behavior. If the assessment of parental behavior is correct, remediation results in changes in the assessed problems of the child.

The general goals of behavioral parent training are: 1) training in observational skills and assessment; 2) formal training in learning theory concepts; 3) application of these concepts to their children; 4) usually, some type of program evaluation to determine the effectiveness of the intervention. To deal with specific goals of the behavioral model, it is necessary to treat the major concepts and techniques used, since mastery and application are the central goal of the model.

## Observation

A review of the literature reveals that most of the didactic materials and reports of practical interventions with single families and groups of families start with comments or emphasis on the importance of learning and how learning relates to human behavior. This type of opening quickly presents basic assumptions of the model to parents. The first concept most sources present is the importance of observation and recording of behaviors. There is a concentrated effort to construct operational definitions of behavior so that parents no longer respond to global concerns such as "Johnny has a bad attitude" but rather focus on how many times Johnny engages in specific observable behaviors such as doing his chores, hitting his little sister, complying with requests, throwing tantrums, initiating arguments at the table, and completing school assignments on time. At this point parents are presented with deficits, excesses and maintenance problems as the major focus of evaluation. Most programs require that parents select a specific behavior and record its occurrence and/or non-occurrence. This data collection procedure ranges from a very thorough and scientific one requiring a number of training sessions to approaches considerably less systematic.

The goal of observing and recording behavior is to determine the strength of a given response. Once the strength of a response is determined, the parent has a standard by which to measure change. If the strength changes in the desired direction, the program is successful. The strength of the target response can be measured a number of ways: frequency of response, duration of response, resistance to extinction, etc., with the simple frequency count the method preferred.

### Functional Analysis of Behavior

Another concept relating to evaluation, the experimental or functional analysis of behavior, is typically presented early in training. This is best described as looking at the antecedents of a given behavior, the behavior itself and the consequences of the behavior. It is an attempt to determine the stimuli that trigger, follow, and may maintain a response. If a pleasant event or the removal of an unpleasant event follows a response, that response is likely to occur again in that setting. If a particular event typically precedes a target response, it may serve as a signal that a pleasant event will follow if the target response is emitted. As an example of functional analysis the following anecdote is broken down and presented in the three column form suggested by Bijou, Peterson and Ault (1968):

> Setting: Mrs. Jones in discount store with Johnnie (age 5). Mrs. Jones and Johnnie walk past a table with small plastic trucks. Johnnie says, "I want a truck." Mrs. Jones says, "No, you can't have one. You have a hundred like that at home already." Mrs. Jones walks on. Johnnie stays by the table and starts to cry. Mrs. Jones returns and says, "OK, if you have to have one, I can't stand to see you cry." They walk on with Johnnie holding the truck and smiling. Johnnie spots another table only this one has a stack of bags full of candy. Johnnie says, "I want candy." Mom says "No." Johnnie starts to cry. Mom grabs the candy and says, "OK, but wait till I tell your father about this."

| Antecedent | Behavior | Consequence |
|---|---|---|
| 1. Johnnie sees truck. | 2. Johnnie says, "I want." | 3. Mother says, "No." |
| 3. Mother says, "No." | 4. Johnnie cries. | 5. Mother gives in. |
| 6. Johnnie sees candy. | 7. Johnnie says he wants it. | 8. Mother says, "No." |
| 8. Mother says, "No." | 9. Johnnie cries. | 10. Mother gives in. |

This example is clearly oversimplified but demonstrates the utility of a functional analysis of behavior. We see that Johnnie's crying is followed by a consequence reinforcing to him. He is likely to repeat the behavior whenever he: 1) sees something, 2) requests it, 3) has his request turned down, 4) then begins to cry and 5) has his wish granted. This three column table can help parents see the relationship between their responses and their children's.

## Reinforcement, Punishment, and Extinction

Parents learn the concepts of reinforcing and punishing behavior, the effects of each, when to use them, and problems in their use or misuse. Parents discover that their own attention, even though they may view it as a punishment when they are critical or negative with a child, may maintain a target response and thus be classified as a reinforcer. Social interaction as a reinforcer and withdrawal of attention as an extinguisher of a response maintained by attention are stressed. Parents are encouraged to seek out as many reinforcement possibilities as possible and seldom resort to the "M and M's" commonly associated with behavior modification.

Four Major Ways of Changing the Strength
of a Given Response

| Procedure | Change in response |
|---|---|
| 1. Add a positive reinforcer after the response | Strengthens |
| 2. Take away or allow to avoid an aversive event | Strengthens |
| 3. Add a punisher or aversive event | Weakens |
| 4. Take away a positive reinforcer | Weakens |

These four change procedures plus modeling are, when combined with the functional analysis of behavior, the major components of the behavioral "bag of tricks."

There are many more concepts, techniques and issues involved, but these four and their correct application are the major concerns of parent trainers (Kazdin, 1975).

## Clear Signals

Central in most parent training programs is emphasis on parents' developing better communication skills. Parents often fail to communicate rules and requests directly. Without clear communication, the parents' lack of verbal influence on the child becomes readily apparent. According to behavioral techniques, parents must reestablish the influence of their verbalizations by pairing them with appropriate reinforcements and punishment. This pairing establishes the power of influence in the parents' directions, reprimands, and positive comments (Bernal, Duryee, Pruett & Burns, 1969).

## Contingency Contracting and Token Economies

Contingency contracting is an agreement between two people that each will deliver something the other values. The agreement specifies some type of social exchange. Behavioral parent training programs encourage contingency contracts in which the parent agrees to provide something the child identifies as a reinforcer, if the child meets a behavioral goal. The idea is simple, but negotiating a fair contract is often complicated. Homme, Casanyi, Gonzales, & Rechs (1969) and Stuart (1971) give examples of this technique.

Token economies are mentioned in a number of parent training references (Alvord, 1973; and Walker & Buckley, 1974). They involve a token given immediately after a desired response. The token can be exchanged later for a more common reinforcer or reinforcing event. The rationale behind using tokens instead of the actual reinforcer is as follows.

1. it may be impossible to dispense certain reinforcers at the time the desired response takes place.
2. tokens can help bridge the temporal gap between a desired response and delayed reinforcement.
3. tokens approximate the "real" world in which people earn tokens (money) to trade for such reinforcers as food, clothing, and pleasant events.
4. the use of tokens specifies the task of the person desiring the modification. This person must focus on the desired behavior and in a sense "catch" the target person being "good," a more positive orientation than catching a child being bad.

### Program Generalization and Program Maintenance

Most parent training programs set up a system to help parents and children expand their newly developed skills. Experiments in learning indicate that often reponses learned in a specific setting take place later only in that setting. Generalization is not a certainty and must be built into the program. The goal of training is that parents apply their new knowledge to other settings and children, and to new behaviors.

The continuation of the child or parent's newly developed behavior must be built into the system to allow for built-in program obsolescence. Very few behavior modifiers or parents plan to have a given behavioral intervention last forever. The program is a temporary environmental change that can keep a behavior going until the consequences available in the environment can maintain it. These natural reinforcers can be either external to the individual or internalized ones such as, "I am doing a better job with the kids," and, "It seems to make dad happy when I do this."

### Program Evaluation

Evaluation techniques assess response strength. If the strength of a target response changes in the desired direction, then the program is seen as effective. More complex procedures can be used to rule out serendipitous changes, but these are beyond the scope of this chapter. Interested readers are referred to Kazdin (1975).

## TRAINING PROCEDURES

Even though the mystique around behavior modification includes impressions of precision problem solving, this is not the case in real life. Such precision and adherence to scientific principles would result in explicit, replicable training procedures. Johnson and Katz (1973) evaluated over 40 behavioral parent training studies, reviewing number of subjects, adequacy of description, primary training techniques, reliability estimates of observations of the target behavior, demonstration of control of the behavior, follow-up, and therapist time investment. Sixteen of the studies were rated as vague in their descriptions of parent training operations, 29 as giving clear instructions. The current authors reviewed the same studies and think Johnson and Katz were very generous in their evaluation since a common discussion of training procedures is summed up in the sentence: "The parents were instructed in the basic principles of operant conditioning and observing behavior." Most training involves some basic didactic instruction by the experimenter, possibly a text or reading material, demonstration of procedures and, occasionally, arrangements for cueing procedures so parents know what to do in a specific setting.

## Didactic Instruction

Didactic training seems a bit incongruous with the behavioral approach, and there is some evidence that it is less effective than modeling and self-observation (Lamb, 1970). Behavior modifiers know that telling children what to do without some program of reinforcement often has little effect on behavior. The same holds true for instructing parents. Yet programmed reinforcement is rarely used.

Reading material ranges from handouts prepared by the parent educator to textbooks of theory and case studies. Home reading assignments serve as foci of discussion. One such text, a manual by Becker (1971b), is a very complete work accompanied by a manual for group leaders (Becker, 1971a). It follows each concept with notes of caution on applying the technique and comprehension exercises. The text also suggests projects to carry out at home and discuss in group sessions. In ten units, Becker's work covers: Consequences: Reinforcers and Punishers; Kinds of Reinforcers and Punishers; When to Reinforce; Using Stronger Reinforcers; Reinforcement and Punishment in Everyday Life; Why Parents (and Teachers) Goof: The Criticism Trap; How to Reinforce; Punishment: When to, How to, and Why not to, Usually; Reasons, Rules, and Reminders; Your Child's Personality and You. The authors have used this text along with other materials in both single and multiple family projects and it has been well received by parents. Reading materials must be gauged to group members' reading levels and interests.

## Role Playing

Role playing allows parent educators to observe parents' actual behaviors in analogous situations. Refinements can be made in role playing situations until parents master new skills. Once this level is reached, parents are encouraged to try out skills at home and report back on the results. Obviously, role playing is a contrived situation, but it may be more like "the real thing" than just talk. Brockway (1974) cites a number of effective role play examples.

## Modeling

Correct and incorrect responses are a modeling procedure. Another type of modeling in single family parent training occurs when the therapist, after completing a thorough evaluation, demonstrates to parents the correct way of interacting with a child in a specific situation. Typically, parents observe this interaction between therapist and child while in the same room or through a one-way vision screen. Parents then attempt to interact with a child in the manner just demonstrated, after which the therapist judges their performance (Johnson and Brown, 1969).

## Cueing

In cueing, the trainer is in the room with parent and child and observes their interaction. When he or she feels a specific response is required from a parent, the trainer presents a cue such as a light (Johnson and Brown, 1969), a finger signal, or a coded message to prompt the appropriate response. This direct method of instruction has been reported very successful and is the one most used in single family projects, typically in a clinical setting.

In the "bug-in-the-ear" cueing technique the trainee wears a small radio receiver in the ear, receiving directions, suggestions, and promptings directly, without disturbing the child involved. Because of its expense, this technique is beyond most counselors' budgets (Welsh, 1966). A less expensive adaptation of the technique uses the earphone and microphone attachments of a tape recorder. A long extension cord allows the trainer to communicate with the trainee from another room.

## Contingency Contracting

Contingency contracting specifies the behaviors parents will carry out at home in return for consultation from the trainer. This requires that participating parents demonstrate high motivation by carrying out their end of the contract (Eyberg, 1973).

## Videotape Feedback

Videotape is frequently used to record parent-child interaction as a basis for follow-up parent-trainer discussion. This technique has been demonstrated effective (Lamb, 1970; Bernal, Duryee, Pruett, & Burns, 1968). Even though it is used primarily in single family training, it could be applied in group settings also. This technique is used frequently in the training of counselors and other professionals and could easily serve the same purpose in the training of parents. For example, all parents could bring their children to school to record some type of interaction for subsequent feedback. Many school districts have video equipment available. Where such equipment is not available, audio recorders could provide a record for purposes of feedback and evaluation. Tapes could be played to parent groups and all could glean positive and negative examples of parental behavior.

## Outline of a Group Approach to Parent Education Using a Behavioral Model

The following program outline includes materials from various sources and builds on the experience of running several groups and training many single families. Each of seven two hour weekly sessions starts with presentation and summary of basic concepts, followed by a break, review of assignments, and the assignment of the next activity. Leaders demonstrate concepts which parents later role play.

Introduction to the Behavioral Model of Evaluation

1. Too much of something
2. Too little of something
3. Problem of keeping something going

How people learn

1. Add SR+
2. Remove SR–
3. Add SR–
4. Remove SR+
5. Modeling
6. Time Out
7. Extinction
8. Difference between learning and performance
9. Shaping

ASSIGNMENT—get each family to pick a concern and keep an anecdotal record on the issue until the next week.

Breaking down anecdotal record into a three-term contingency table

1. Antecedents of behavior
2. Behaviors well defined
3. Consequences of behavior

Discussion of ways of measuring the strength of a given response

ASSIGNMENT—baseline collection on two concerns

Each family presents baseline data according to a model presented by instructor

Presentation of some of the basic change procedures

Review of "How People Learn"

ASSIGNMENT—continue baselines

| | |
|---|---|
| *Session*<br>*number* | *General conduct* |
| 4 | Review baselines |

Review change procedures

Selection of a change procedure for and by each family

Development of a Grand Plan

  Definition—was the baseline definition appropriate?
  Selection of SR– or SR+ (Premack, Grandma's rule)
  Selection of criteria
  Child included in the contract?
  Specification of contract if a formal contract is used

  ASSIGNMENT—parents carry out Grand Plan
              instructors to follow-up with trouble-
              shooting call after two days

| | |
|---|---|
| *Session*<br>*number* | *General content* |
| 5 | Review and evaluation of Grand Plans |

Modification of Grand Plans

Introduction of the more esoteric concepts such as schedules of reinforcement, modeling, chaining, etc.

Review the difference between learning and performance
  and what issues seem to relate to each

  ASSIGNMENT—continuation of Grand Plans and data
              collection
              start baseline on second concern

| | |
|---|---|
| *Session*<br>*number* | *General content* |
| 6 | Review of Grand Plans |

Introduction of the general problem solving scheme under
  which we have been operating

  1.  Definition of the problem:

        too much?
        too little?
        how to keep it going?
        what happens before?
        what is the real response?
        what happens after?

75

*(Continued)*

   2. Generation of a number of possible interventions—
      some good, some bad, etc.

   3. Selection of Grand Plan

      can it be done?
      is it the simplest way to approach the problems?
      does it create any more problems?
      who is in control of the plan?
      what are some of the possible things that can go
         wrong?
      how do you decide on SR+ and SR−, etc?
      can you get target person involved?
      does target person see it as a problem?

   4. Start Grand Plan

   5. Evaluation of Grand Plan

   Transfer of change

   ASSIGNMENT—starting of second Grand Plan

| *Session number* | *General content* |
|---|---|
| 7 | Playing psychologist-social worker, etc. |

   1. Active listening
   2. Respect for personal opinion
   3. Generous use of reflection and requests for clarifi-
      cation
   4. Introducing the ideas involved in reciprocal Roles and
      social exchange theory
   5. How to deal with fears

   Monitor second Grand Plan

   Arrange for follow-up

(Stern and Lamb, 1975)

## TRAINING OF TRAINERS

The literature on the behavioral approach to parent education does not treat the training of trainers as a specific
topic. The general tone of the literature indicates that ini-

tial theoretical training is followed by more practical training. From the present authors' own experiences, this practical training typically uses single families. Several references, such as Becker (1971a) and Brockway (1974), give concrete suggestions to leaders of parent groups but give very little regarding the requisite skills for a parent educator within the behavioral model.

## RESOURCES

Research Press, 2612 North Mattis Avenue, Champaign, Illinois 61820.

## REFERENCES

Alvord, J. *Home token economy: An incentive program for children and their parents.* Champaign, Ill.: Research Press, 1973.

Becker, W. C. *Guide for group leaders for "parents are teachers: A child management program."* Champaign, Ill.: Research Press, 1971 (a).

Becker, W. C. *Parents are teachers: A child management program.* Champaign, Ill.: Research Press, 1971 (b).

Berkowitz, B. P., & Graziano, A. M. Training parents as behavior therapists: A review. *Behavior Research & Therapy,* 1972, **10** (4), 297–317.

Bernal, M. Behavioral feedback in the modification of brat behaviors. *Journal of Nervous & Mental Disease,* 1968, **148** (4), 375–386.

Bernal, M., Duryee, I. S., Pruett, H. L., & Burns, B. J. Behavior modification and the brat syndromes. *Journal of Consulting and Clinical Psychology,* 1968, **32,** 447–455.

Bijou, S. W., Peterson, R. F., & Ault, M. A method to integrate descriptive and experimental field studies at the level of data and empirical concepts. *Journal of Applied Behavior Analysis,* 1968 1, 175–191.

Breger, L., & McGaugh, J. L. Critique and reformulation of "learning-theory" approaches to psychotherapy and neurosis. *Psychological Bulletin,* 1965, **63,** 338–358.

Brockway, B. S. *Training in child management: A family approach.* Dubuque, Iowa: Kendall/Hunt Pubs., 1974.

Coleman, R. G. A procedure for fading from experimenter-school based to parent-home based control of classroom behavior. *Journal of School Psychology,* 1973, **11,** 71–79.

Cone, J. D., & Sloop, E. W. Parents as agents of change. In A. Jacobs, & W. Spradlin (Eds.), *The group as agent of change.* New York: Behavioral Publications, 1974.

Deibert, A. N., & Harmon, A. J. *New tools for changing behavior.* Champaign, Ill.: Research Press, 1970.

Eyberg, S. M. An outcome study of child family intervention: Effects of contingency contracting and order of treated problems (Doctoral dissertation, University of Oregon, 1972). *Dissertation Abstracts International,* 1973, **33,** 4503B (University Microfilms No. 73–7888).

Fishman, C. A., & Fishman, D. B. A group training program in behavior modification for mothers of children with birth defects. *Child Psychiatry and Human Development*, 1975, **6**, 3–14.

Guerney, B. F. (Ed.). *Psychotherapeutic agents: New roles for nonprofessionals, parents, and teachers*. New York: Holt, Rinehart and Winston, 1969.

Gordon, B. N., & Kogan, K. L. A mother instruction program. *Child Psychiatry and Human Development*, 1975, **6**, 89–106.

Hall, R. V. *Managing behavior* (3 Vols.). Merriam, Kansas: H & H Enterprises, Inc., 1970.

Hawkins, R. P.; Peterson, R. F.; Schweid, E.; & Bijou, S. W. Behavior therapy in the home: Amelioration of problem parent-child relations with the parent in a therapeutic role. *Journal of Experimental Child Psychology*, 1966, **4**, 99–107.

Henderson, R. W., & Garcia, A. B. The effects of parent training on the question-asking behavior of Mexican-American children. *American Educational Research Journal*, 1973, **10**, (3), 193–201.

Herbert, E. W., Pinkston, E. M., Hayden, M. L., Sajwaj, T. E., Pinkston, S., Cordua, G., Jackson, C. Adverse effects of differential parental attention. *Journal of Applied Behavior Analysis*, 1973 **6** (1), 15–30.

Hirsch, I., & Walder, L. Training mothers as reinforcement therapists for their own children. *Proceedings of the 77th Annual Convention of the American Psychological Association*, 1968, **4**, 561–562.

Holland, C. J. An interview guide for behavioral counseling with parents. *Behavior Therapy*, 1970, **1**, 70–79.

Homme, L., Casanyi, A., Gonzales, M., & Rechs, J. How to use contingency contracting in the classroom. Champaign, Ill.: Research Press, 1969.

Johnson, C. A., & Katz, R. C. Using parents as change agents for their own children: A review. *Journal of Child Psychology and Psychiatry*, 1973, **14**, 181–200.

Johnson, S. M., & Brown, R. A. Producing behavior change in parents of disturbed children. *Journal of Child Psychology and Psychiatry*, 1969, **10**, 107–121.

Kazdin, A. E. *Behavior modification in applied settings*. Homewood, Ill.: Dorsey Press, 1975.

Kimmel, H. D., & Kimmel, E. An instrumental conditioning method for the treatment of enuresis. *Journal of Behavior Therapy & Experimental Psychiatry*, 1970, **1**, (2), 121–123.

Kogan, K. L., & Gordon, B. N. A mother-instruction program: Documenting change in mother-child interactions. *Child Psychiatry and Human Development*, 1975, **5**, 189–200.

Kozloff, M. A. *Reaching the autistic child: A parent training program*. Champaign, Ill., Research Press, 1973.

Lamb, W. A. *A comparison of various techniques of training mothers as language-concept models for their children.* Unpublished doctoral dissertation, University of Arizona, 1970.

Lamb, W. A. & Reidy, T. J. *The SOAP system: A proposed model for parent training.* Unpublished manuscript, DePaul University, 1975.

Lebow, M.D. Behavior modification in parent-child therapy: A bibliography. *Catalog of Selected Documents in Psychology,* 1973, **2,** 12–13.

London, P. End of ideology in behavior modification. *American Psychologist,* 1972, **27,** 913–920.

Mash, E. J., Handy, L. C., & Hamerlynck, L. A. *Behavior Modification Approaches to Parenting.* New York: Bruner/Mazel, 1976.

Mash, E. J., Handy, L. C., & Hamerlynck, L. A. *Behavior Modification and Families.* New York: Bruner/Mazel, 1976.

Mash, E. J., Lazers, R., Terdal, L., & Garner, A. Modification of mother-child interactions: A modeling approach for groups. *Child Study Journal,* 1973 **3,** 131–143.

Mathis, H. Training a "disturbed" boy using the mother as therapist: A case study. *Behavior Therapy,* 1971, **2,** 233–239.

McIntire, R. W. *For love of children: Behavioral psychology for parents.* Del Mar, Cal.: C. R. M. Books, Inc., 1970.

Mira, M. Results of a behavior modification training program for parents and teachers. *Behavior Research & Therapy,* 1970, **8** (3), 309–311.

Mira, M. Behavior modication applied to training young deaf children. *Exceptional Children,* 1972, **39** (3), 225–229.

Moustakas, C. E. & Makowsky, G. Client-centered therapy with parents. *Journal of Consulting Psychology,* 1952, **16,** 338–342.

Neisworth, J. T. & Moore, F. Operant treatment of asthmatic responding with the parent as therapist. *Behavior Therapy,* 1972, **3,** 95–99.

O'Dell, S. Training parents in behavior modification. *Psychological Bulletin,* 1974, **81,** 418–433.

Patterson, G. R. *Families: Applications of social learning to family life.* Champaign, Ill.: Research Press, 1971.

Patterson, G. R. Reprogramming the families of aggressive boys. In C. R. Thoresen (Ed.), *Behavior modification in education: I.* Chicago: National Society for the Study of Education, 1972.

Patterson, G. R. & Guillion, M. E. *Living with children: New methods for parents and teachers.* Champaign, Ill.: Research Press, 1971.

Pumroy, D. K. *A new approach to treating parent-child problems.* Paper presented at the meeting of the American Psychological Association, New York, 1965. (Available from D. K. Pumroy, University of Maryland, College Park, Md. 20740.)

Salzinger, K., Feldman, R. S., & Portnoy, S. Training parents of brain-injured children in the use of operant conditioning procedures. *Behavior Therapy*, 1970, 1 (1), 4–32.

Schaefer, J. W., Palkes, H. S., & Stewart, M. A. Group counseling for parents of hyperactive children. *Child Psychiatry and Human Development*, 1974, 5, 89–94.

Shack, J. R., & Barnett, L. W. *An annotated and indexed bibliography of behavior management with children*. 1973. (Available from J. R. Shack, Loyola University of Chicago.)

Shah, S. A. Training and utilizing a mother as the therapist for her child. In B. G. Guerney (Ed.), *Psychotherapeutic agents: New roles for nonprofessionals, parents and teachers*. New York: Holt, Rinehart and Winston, 1969.

Smith, J. M., & Smith, D. E. P. *Child management: A program for parents*. Ann Arbor, Michigan: Ann Arbor Pubs., 1966.

Stern, S. B., & Lamb, W. A. *Outline for parent education project. (Unpublished manuscript available from S. B. Stern, Institute for Juvenile Research, 907 S. Wolcott, Chicago, Ill., 1975).*

Stuart, R. Behavioral contracting with the families of delinquents. *Journal of Behavior Therapy and Experimental Psychiatry*, 1971, 2, 1–11.

Stumphauzer, J. S. A Low-cost "bug-in-the-ear" sound system for modification of therapist, parent and patient behavior. *Behavior Therapy*, 1971, 2 (2), 249–250.

Tahmisian, J. A., & McReynolds, W. T. Use of parents as behavioral engineers in the treatment of a school-phobic girl. *Journal of Counseling Psychology*, 1971, 18 (3), 225–228.

Tavormina, J. B. Relative effectiveness of behavioral and reflective group counseling with parents of mentally retarded children. *Journal of Consulting and Clinical Psychology*, 1975, 43, 22–31.

Tavormina, J. B. Basic models of parent counseling: A critical review. *Psychological Bulletin*, 1974, 81, 827–835.

Terdal, L. & Buell, J. Parent education in managing retarded children with behavior deficits and inappropriate behaviors. *Mental Retardation*, 1967, 7 (3), 10–13.

Valett, R. E. *Modifying children's behavior: A guide for parents and professionals*. Palo Alto Cal.: Fearon Publishers, 1969.

Wagner, M. K. Parent therapist: An operant conditioning method. *Mental Hygiene*, 1968, 52, 452–455.

Wahler, R. G., Winkel, G. H., Peterson, R. E., & Morrison, D. C. Mothers as behavior therapists for their own children. *Behavior Research and Therapy*, 1965, 3, 113–124.

Walker, H. M., & Buckley, N. K. *Token reinforcement techniques.* Eugene, Ore.: E-B Press, 1974.

Walter, H. I., & Gilmore, S. L. Placebo versus social learning effects in parent training procedures designed to alter the behavior of aggressive boys. *Behavior Therapy,* 1973, **4,** 361–377.

Watson, L. A. *Child behavior modification: A manual for teachers, nurses and parents.* New York: Pergamon Press, Inc., 1973.

Welsh, R. S. *A highly efficient method of parental counseling.* Paper presented at the meeting of the Rocky Mountain Psychological Association, 1966.

Wetzel, R. J., Baker, J., Roney, M. & Martin, M. Outpatient treatment of autistic behavior. *Behavior Research and Therapy,* 1966, **4,** 169–177.

Wittes, G., & Radin, N. *The reinforcement approach: Helping your child to learn.* San Rafael, Cal.: Dimensions Pub. Co., 1969.

Zeilberger, J., Sampen, S. E., & Sloan, H. N. Modification of a child's problem behaviors in the home with the mother as the therapist. *Journal of Applied Behavior Analysis,* 1968, **1,** 47–54.

Included in this chapter are the principles of rational emotive therapy and their suggested applications in parent education.

*Chapter 5*

# RATIONAL EMOTIVE THERAPY MODEL

## HISTORY AND PRINCIPLES

This particular theory of helping people began with Dr. Albert Ellis. From his experiences and study it became apparent to him that people could be taught to approach their problems from a rational, logical point of view.

The central theme of R.E.T., according to Ellis (1970), is that:

> . . . man is a uniquely rational as well as a uniquely irrational animal, that his emotional or psychological disturbances are a result of his thinking illogically or irrationally; and that he can rid himself of most of his emotional or mental unhappiness, ineffectuality and disturbance if he learns to maximize his rational thinking and minimize his irrational thinking [p.36].

Ellis believes that most people giving therapy are teaching their clients to reperceive and rethink the events and experiences of their lives. R.E.T. is based on the belief that people are not only indoctrinated with irrational, mistaken ideas of their own worthlessness when they are young, but also that they hold onto these into their adult lives. The therapist's job then is to show clients:

1.  How their difficulties result from distorted perception and illogical thinking.
2.  A relatively simple method of reordering their perceptions and reorganizing their thinking to remove the basic causes of their difficulties.

Another belief Ellis offers is that rarely, if ever, do we experience any of life's four operations (sensing, moving, emoting, and thinking) in isolation. In other words, thoughts and emotions overlap.

Rational emotive therapy cites eleven major illogical and irrational ideas which cause people difficulties (Ellis, 1962):

1.  It is a dire necessity for an adult human being to be loved or approved by virtually every *significant other* person he or she knows.
2.  One should be thoroughly compentent, adequate, and achieving in all possible respects to consider oneself worthwhile.
3.  Certain people are wicked and should be severely blamed and punished for their villainy.
4.  It is awful and catastrophic when things are not the way one wants them to be.
5.  Human happiness is externally caused; people have little or no control over their sorrows and disturbances.
6.  If something is or may be dangerous or fearsome one should be terribly concerned about it and dwell on the possibility of its occurring.
7.  It is easier to avoid than to face certain life difficulties and self-responsibilities.
8.  One should be dependent on others and rely on someone stronger than oneself.

9.  One's past history is an all-important determiner of present behavior; because something once strongly affected one's life, it should indefinitely have a similar effect.
10. One should become quite upset over other people's problems and disturbances.
11. There is invariably a right, precise, and perfect solution to human problems, and it is catastrophic if this perfect solution is not found [pp. 61–68].

## GOALS

Hauck (1972) points out that all that is needed to solve problems is to identify false ideas, then use logic to show and hopefully convince a client of the ideas' irrationality. Once a child acquires new knowledge in this way, parents must encourage him or her to behave differently. R.E.T. programs familiarize parents with Ellis's eleven points. Counselors want to be certain that parents are skilled in logical thinking practices. Parents need some time to orient themselves to this philosophy—which appears to be so simple. Another learning task for the parents is familiarization with the list of Hauck's "Erroneous Beliefs of Child Management."

Counselors also work toward the goal of familiarization with the special tactics Hauck lists. Parents ultimately would be able to use the R.E.T. approach not only to raise emotionally sound, happy children but to help themselves feel less guilty about their child rearing practices.

## TRAINING PROCEDURES

None of the R.E.T. literature specifies procedures for parent education, addressing itself instead to the principles and their application. We take the liberty throughout this section of suggesting possible methods for implementation and organization.

As stated above, rational emotive counseling is based on people remaining rational and logical about events and circumstances. For parents this seems quite difficult at first and it is probably the opposite of their current practices and habits. Therefore, we suggest at least ten 90 minute training sessions to fully develop each concept and to practice or role play some situations.

Suggestions for working with parents can be found by extending Ellis' experiences with groups, some of which were with families. He found that:

1.   Group members have other members/participants to feed back how irrational the self-indoctrinations really are.

2.   Group members act as counselors to each other as they more clearly see their own difficulties.

3.   Sometimes just hearing others' problems is beneficial.

4.   One parent's solution to a problem helps other parents.

5.   Sometimes parents see something first in others, which they later see in themselves.

6.   Assignments for homework are carried out better when suggested and assigned by the group itself.

7.   More hypotheses are offered since there are more participants.

Parents are not put into a pressure, "true confession" situation but rather are encouraged by the counselors and other group members to speak up. As in other models, the counselor must work toward making parents unafraid to discuss difficulties with their children.

What is it we are going to teach these parents? First, counselors have to concentrate on the underlying principles discussed earlier in this chapter, since parents need a good understanding of these principles before proceeding.

Next presented would be the "Erroneous Beliefs of Child Management" as described by Hauck (1972).

1. Children Must Not Question or Disagree with Their Superiors.
   a. Some disagreement is good as parents could be wrong.
   b. Our children do not think less of us just because they disapprove of our thinking.
   c. A child's silence does not mean agreement.
   d. A child is not thinking for himself.
   e. We might be asking a child to be untruthful.
   f. We might create guilt.
   g. Forbidding disareement denies the ability to reason, which is an essential tool for control of our emotions.
2. A Child and His/Her Behavior are the Same.
   a. Parents must separate their children from the children's acts.
   b. Parents must accept the fact that we are all human and humans aren't perfect.
   c. Objectionable behavior occurs because of low intelligence, ignorance or lack of skill, and emotional disturbance.
3. Children Can Upset Their Superiors.
   a. We as parents upset ourselves.
   b. We must learn to ask ourselves, "What did I say to myself just before I became upset?"
   c. We upset ourselves when we believe it is *necessary* to have well-behaved children.
   d. We confuse desires with needs.
4. Punishment, Guilt, and Blame are Effective Methods of Child Management.

    a.  Parents must be sure that the discipline does not become a new crime.

    b.  Undesirable behavior must become desirable in some new way.

    c.  The child's inward thinking must change as well as his/her outward behavior.

    d.  Demand perfection and you will have a tense child.

    e.  Correcting with anger builds resentment and hatred in the child.

    f.  These tend to create emotional disturbance and misconduct.

5.  Children Learn More from What Their Superiors Say than from What They Do.

    a.  Learning occurs when we practice what we preach.

    b.  If parents seldom get angry over frustrations, children then see that the control of emotion works.

6.  Praise Spoils a Child.

    a.  Praise the act not the child.

    b.  Praise acts as a reward and strengthens the behavior.

    c.  A child feels good about himself or herself.

    d.  Lack of control spoils children, not praise.

    e.  Less harm is done by overpraising than by underpraising.

7.  Children Must Not Be Frustrated.

    a.  It will make adult life seem more frustrating if children are protected from frustration during childhood.

    b.  Children are bored without some problems and challenges.

    c.  Children must learn to avoid unnecessary frustrations, remove or minimize problems after they arise and to accept what they cannot change.

8. Heavy Penalties Work Best if Applied First.
   a. Undue punishment breeds contempt.
   b. After all, if things can't get any worse, why behave correctly?
   c. Severe punishment can work too well and make a child fearful of all situations.
9. A Child Must Earn His/Her Parents' Love.
   a. Do not withhold love for misbehavior.
   b. Love as payment is hard on the learning process; the child is in an all or nothing situation.
10. Children Should be Calmed First, Adults Second.
    a. Adults should calm themselves first in order to be effective teachers.
    b. If adults are not calm the child's behavior will only increase. [p. 14–38].

After pursuing each of these incorrect beliefs, the reasoning behind them and the results of such actions, parents practice and discuss how they apply to their situations. A counselor may focus on undesirable habits of children, fears of children, anger, etc. as topics for discussion.

When sessions are almost complete it is good to cover Hauck's instructions to parents. In brief they are:

1. Do not change your tactics just because they do not produce immediate results.

2. Penalize misbehavior which is a reaction to a penalty.

3. Tantrums and acting out look worse than they really are.

4. Misbehavior will often worsen before it gets better.

5. Our being upset is their reward.

6. Only be concerned with some of the child's frustrations.

7.   Practically all parents have some regret that they are parents.

8.   Experiment if you want—parental mistakes are seldom fatal.

9.   Remember, your child should be praised more than criticized.

This should be helpful to parents as they begin to apply R.E.T. principles on their own. Knaus (1975) says that guidance counselors can save much time by using a system which goes directly to the irrational heart of problems, using words and methods which are familiar to all concerned. This should provide some added encouragement to counselors to try this model of parent education.

## RESOURCES

Institute for Rational Living, Inc., 45 East 65th Street, New York, New York 10021.

*Rational Living,* published by the Institute for Rational Living, 45 East 65th Street, New York, New York 10021.

## REFERENCES

Ellis, A. *Reason and emotion in psychotherapy.* New York: Lyle Stuart, 1962.

Ellis, A. *How to live with a neurotic.* New York: Crown Publishers, 1957.

Hauck, P. A. *The rational management of children.* New York: Libra Publishers, 1972.

Knaus, W. I. Manuscript accepted for publication in *Rational Living,* 1975, **9.**

Knaus, W. I. *Rational emotive education: A manual for elementary school teachers.* New York: Institute for Rational Living, 1974.

Lantz, J. E. The rational treatment of parental adjustment reaction to adolescence. *Clinical Social Work Journal,* 1975, **3,** 100–108.

Several models of parent education, mental health related interventions, and examples of parent training are presented in this chapter. The material in this chapter may be very useful to a parent educator but has not included specifics on parent education or on the training procedures involved. Psychoanalytic models (including the Child Study Association of American and Transactional Analysis), reality therapy, Haim Ginott and pre-school examples are reviewed.

*Chapter 6*

# ADDITIONAL MODELS AND USE OF PARENT EDUCATION

## PSYCHOANALYTIC

### *History and Basic Assumptions*

There are several models or approaches to parent training that do not fit into the models listed previously in this monograph and remain distinct enough in their approach to separate them from the eclectic models. The psychoanalytic approach fits this category. The basic psychoanalytic approach to psychotherapy and the study of personality is based more on a medical model rather than on an educational model. Psychoanalysis is a relearning experience in which patients learn about their emotional states and the connections between them, their reactions to these states and to external events. The theoretical orientation emphasizes the importance of unconscious processes in this relearning. Education, viewed from the psychoanalytic point of view, is a conscious process. Hence, education of patients (and/or parents) is basically outside the territory of classical psychoanalysis.

In spite of the lack of congruence between classical psychoanalysis and parent education, it is interesting to note that one of Freud's first cases involved training a parent to carry out the psychoanalysis of his child, "Little Hans," who had a fear of horses. Freud carried out the treatment by serving as consultant to the boys's father (Freud, 1950). This training of a parent in psychoanalytic techniques is clearly within the range of "therapy," while many behavioral models of training parents as therapists fall more within the educational realm.

## CHILD STUDY ASSOCIATION OF AMERICA

### History

One of the most extensive examples of parent education in the literature is the program of the Child Study Association of America (CSAA). The history, purposes, philosophy, and programs of this association are clearly described in two sources: *Parents Learn Through Discussion: Principles and Practices of Parent Group Education* by Aline B. Auerbach (1968) and *Education for Child Rearing* by Orville G. Brim (1959). Both sources indicate that when the Child Study Association of America was founded during the 1880's, its function was to meet the needs of what appears to have been a group of middle class, well educated mothers who wanted to study experts' opinions on child rearing. From this rather clearly traditional educational beginning, the CSAA staff began to realize that parents needed to understand not only their children's needs but their own needs as well. The group discussion format was developed as a means to help parents find out more about themselves. Over the years these parent groups, as outlined by Auerbach and Brim, developed a philosophy and style that is farily consistent with the psychoanalytic view of human development. Several of the most influential consultants to the program were psychoanalysts. Further support for classifying the CSAA program as psychoanalytically oriented derives from the description by Auerbach (1968) of the skills needed by group leaders. She states, "This knowledge should be based on the psychodynamic point of view, and should include a sensitive awareness of the 'language of behavior'—the meanings, manifestations, and etiology of behavior in general and particularly in the family [p. 162]." She adds, however, that in no way does a group leader attempt to elicit "forgotten or unconscious" material. This avoidance of direct attempts at focusing on unconscious material is a major distinction between psychoanalysis and psychoanalytically oriented parent education.

Basic assumptions maintained by the CSAA program in addition to psychodynamic assumptions are outlined by Auerbach (1968) as follows:

1. Parents can learn.
2. Parents want to learn.
3. Parents learn best what they are interested in learning.
4. Learning is most significant when the subject matter is closely related to the parents' own immediate experience with their children.
5. Parents can learn best when they are free to create their own response to a situation.
6. Parent group education is as much an emotional experience as it is an intellectual one.
7. Parents can learn from one another.
8. Parent group education provides the basis for remaking experience.
9. Each parent learns his or her own way [pp. 23–28].

Of these basic assumptions, numbers 6 and 8 most closely identify the approach as related to a psychoanalytic model.

## Goals

The goals of the CSAA can be inferred directly from a number of the above assumptions. A major goal of the

CSAA parent education program is to develop and use a program based on both sound practice and sound philosophy. Auerbach warns that her book is not the typical handbook but one presenting a philosophy along with some practical experience. Accordingly, the goals of the program are not easily enumerated in a short list. The program expects parents to become more aware of their children's developmental stages and the needs particularly important at each stage. Parents are expected to evaluate themselves in terms of what their own goals are as parents. They are expected to observe how their goals relate to previous experience and become more aware of interactions that take place in the family setting. The final area of expected personal and parental growth is an increased appreciation for the large number of events and circumstances that directly influence both child and parent.

### Training and Training of Trainers

The sole technique of parent education is group discussion. Hence, group dynamics and group processes are key issues in training. The basic assumptions of the CSAA program evince the belief that the medium is the message. The group helps select agenda topics, supports and encourages individual members, and sets an atmosphere of "we are all in this thing together and have common concerns." The training methods are so entwined with the philosophy and goals that readers are directed to the original sources if, after brief exposure, they have an interest in this model of training. This model of training is very much like the model for training professional social workers.

The Child Study Association of America provides this training program in the New York area and in other areas as well. CSAA training focuses on child development, group processes, and dynamically oriented approaches to studying humans. The Association typically provides direct consultation and supervision of trainees when they run their initial groups.

## TRANSACTIONAL ANALYSIS

### History and Basic Assumptions

Transactional analysis is another model of intervention linked directly to the psychoanalytic framework. Berne (1961), describing transactional analysis, discusses three ego states that can be determined by what he calls "structural analysis." This structural analysis involves the separation or segregation of the Parent, Adult, and Child ego states. The Parent ego state involves those aspects of a person dealing with prescriptions and proscriptions. When a man's inner language tells him that he should or should not do something, his Parent is in control. The Adult ego state functions rationally and tests reality. When a woman's inner language is functioning much like a computer, checking facts, updating data, comparing bits of information and input, her Adult is in control. The Child ego state involves fears and desires. When a man's inner language tells him he would like to do a given act even though it might be forbidden, then the Child is functioning.

Berne (1961) indicates that in many ways these ego states are different from the psychoanalytic constructs of superego, ego, and id, respectively. To the uninitiated, however, the states appear extremely similar.

### Goals

Proponents of Transactional Analysis (TA) focus on two activities—structural analysis as outlined above, and transactional analysis. Transactional analysis examines the transactions between individuals. These transactions are analyzed on the basis of the ego states of each of the persons involved in the interchange. A person acts from within a given ego state when attempting to communicate with another person. That communication is addressed to a particular ego state in the other person. As Berne (1972) points out, when two people contact one another six ego states may be involved. When only two ego states are involved in the total exchange, the transaction is complementary. This type of exchange can be made repeatedly since it meets the communications needs of the parties involved. An example of this type of communication is given by Harris (1967) along with the following diagram to indicate the parallel lines showing the complementary nature of the exchange:

A man on a bus asks the driver if they will arrive at their destination on time. The bus driver replies that they will arrive on time.

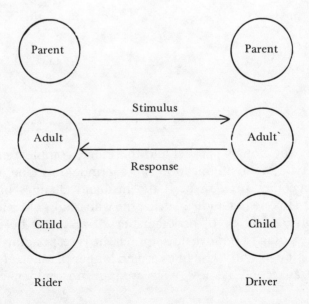

The flow was parallel. The rider acted from his adult ego state by indicating a desire for information. The driver replied from his adult ego state with a direct response to a direct question. Yet another complementary transaction can be seen in the following example (Harris, 1967):

A wife requests that her husband remove a dead mouse from a trap because she is so frightened by mice. The husband complies with this request because he is big and strong and needs to take care of the little woman.

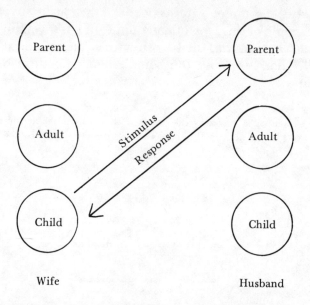

Again, the flow is parallel and therefore, complementary. This type of communication can continue until one member becomes tired of it. If the husband changes his response to one that indicates that the wife is now old enough to solve this type of problem herself and that he is no longer going to remove mice for her, he is responding from a parent ego state. The lines are no longer parallel. Hence, the transaction is now a crossed or uncomplementary transaction and communication is disrupted. The example of the husband refusing his wife's request would be diagrammed as follows:

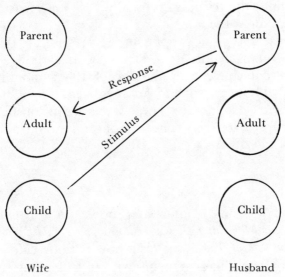

Wife                                    Husband

Transactional analysis also implies a more thorough evaluation of the forms of social action. Berne (1972) indicates that there are six basic types of social behavior available when two people interact:

1. Withdrawal—with no overt communication.
2. Rituals—signs of mutual recognition, strokes.
3. Activities—work, externally oriented toward the task.
4. Pastimes—repetitive interchanges, socially programmed.
5. Games—interactions with hidden ulterior motives where both parties collect some type of payoff.
6. Intimacy—game-free, candid exchanges.

In addition to these basic types of social actions, scripts or life plans are a central concept in TA. The six forms of social action listed above are ways to structure short periods of time; the script is essentially a person's master plan for spending a lifetime.

Berne and other proponents of TA indicate that children develop all three ego states at an early age. They suggest that children by the age of 10–12 months have developed both Parent and Adult ego states in addition to their obvious Child state. These states are in constant flux. Children develop ego states by observing and modeling parents and others.

### Training

James (1974), in an interesting book titled *Transactional Analysis for Moms and Dads: What Do You Do with Them Now That You've Got Them,* suggests how parents can use TA concepts in evaluating themselves and their interactions with their children. By determining the ego states involved in an exchange with their child, parents better understand communication and communication breakdown. The book is written for professionals and parents but includes no specific suggestions for parent educators to use in assisting parents with transactional analysis. James and Jongeward (1971) present a number of specific suggestions and exercises combining TA and Gestalt concepts that would be useful in work with parents.

### Training of Trainers

Most training of professionals in the use of TA techniques is conducted outside the standard graduate programs for counselors. There are several institutes at which people can receive training by certified TA instructors. In addition, TA workshops often accompany various professional meetings. For more information on TA training, James (1974) suggest the following addresses:

> International Transactional Analysis Association
> 3155 College Avenue
> Berkeley, California 94705

> and

> Transactional Analysis Institute
> Box 356
> Lafayette, California 94549

## REALITY THERAPY

### History

This approach to counseling and therapy was initiated by William Glasser, M.D. When he was finishing his training in psychiatry, it became apparent to him that the medical model of therapy was not successful. He noted the years needed for therapy, the patients who never leave the hospital, and those who keep returning to therapy.

### Basic Assumptions

Glasser (1965) describes reality therapy as leading a person toward dealing successfully with the real world. A therapist must be able not only to help patients accept the real world, but to help them fulfill their needs in it. It is Glasser's belief that most people enter therapy because they are not having some of their needs fulfilled. To fulfill our needs we must:

1. Be involved with other people.
2. Love and be loved.
3. Feel we are worthwhile to ourselves and others.

Glasser (1965) defines responsibility as "the ability to fulfill one's needs and to do so in a way that does not deprive others of the ability to fulfill their needs [p. 13]." A patient must come to see that he/she is responsible for personal behavior, and that the therapist will be more concerned with behavior than with attitudes. Reality therapy does not look at past history, does not accept excuses for deviant behavior and does not focus on unconscious thinking. "Why?" is rarely asked in reality therapy. The concern is more, "What are you doing?"

## Training Procedures

Glasser does not apply his model of therapy to parent education, yet it appears to be a model which could be used. Reality therapy focuses on educating people to new ways of living and does not see patients as being sick. It teaches responsibility and caring for yourself and others. All of the above characteristics would help build a good model for parent education.

A parent education program could assume that:

1.   Parents are responsible for their own behavior.
2.   Parents can teach children to be responsible for their own behavior.
3.   All family members can come to love themselves and each other.
4.   Parents and children can learn to accept reality and to seek to have their needs fulfilled in the real world.

## PRE-SCHOOL PROGRAMS

### History

Legislation efforts in the 1960's prompted much discussion of early development of children. Most educators, mental health specialists and child care workers expressed the opinion that more funding and attention should be focused on children at younger ages. Many expectations were raised concerning improved reading abilities and language skills, better adjusted teens and happier adults, if early school programs were developed.

With legislation came dollars for pre-school programs such as Head Start and Project Follow Through. Many innovative school programs were developed for primary grade children (K-3). Early in the development of these programs it became clear that parents needed to be involved and that parent involvement should occur at the earliest possible time. Almost all of the work in early child-parent intervention has been done with minority and economically disadvantaged families.

## Training Procedures

Most efforts in this area of parent education can be subsumed under one of three types:

1. Training mothers at school to work in the classroom.
2. Training mothers at school or agency for home application.
3. Training mothers at home.

All of the above categories were implemented in groups and on an individual basis. They can be further divided into major goal classifications. Some projects' goals were to teach parents better management procedures with their children. Other projects' goals were to teach parents to encourage and stimulate learning while their children were very young.

Techniques included:

1. Teaching mothers how to observe behavior in a classroom which they could eventually use at home as well.
2. Teaching mothers how to teach at school.
3. Using structured language patterns to improve verbal abilities.
4. Using toys to teach important concepts such as colors, shapes, vocabulary.
5. Showing mothers through video tape, role playing and demonstrations how to praise, encourage and reward.
6. Using mothers to train mothers.
7. Printed materials for mothers to read.

Many programs were reported as being effective (Costello & Binstock, 1970; Fenichel, 1966; Gordon, 1968). Few were able to show "hard data" of their work with mothers. Nevertheless, the literature is rich with examples of work with families who are not represented in the other models. In addition many authors point out errors made as well as what appeared to be successful. The bulk of parent education work has been in pre-school and early childhood programs and provides a good basis for elementary counselors planning programs.

## HAIM GINOTT

Haim Ginott has exerted a great influence in parent education. His book, *Between Parent & Child* (1965), has been read by thousands of parents and professionals. He maintains his approach is based almost solely on the skills of communicating. He tells parents they must learn "Childrenese."

This new way of communicating is based on respect and skill. It requires that:

1. Messages preserve the child's and parent's self-respect.

2. Statements of advice or instruction must be preceded by statements of understanding.

In other words, parents must learn to hear the feelings behind what a child is saying and reflect those to him. For example:

Child:   I'm never going to school again.

Parent:   You had a terrible day at school today.

Child:   Boy, did I ever.

When the parent didn't respond by saying, "Oh, yes, you are going to back to school," the child was more able to converse calmly and rationally about his time at school. For too long people have been educated out of really knowing their own feelings. For this reason it is difficult for parents to recognize even their own feelings and more difficult for them to hear the child's. So often when people say they hate someone, others tell them they really only dislike that person. Ginott suggests that this is dishonest and adults must help children know what they feel.

Basically there are three goals for parents in this method. They are:

1. Listening with sensitivity.
   a. Parents who are attentive to what their children are saying show the children that their ideas are valued.
   b. Children gain a sense of self-worth.
2. Preventing "grapes of wrath."
   a. Avoid messages that create hate or resentment.
   b. Avoid insults, name calling, prophesizing, threats, accusations, bossing.

3. Stating feelings and thoughts without attacking.
   a. Parents should say what they honestly feel.
   b. Avoid attacking the child as a person.

In addition, parents should allow children to learn how to make decisions. There is a distinction made between allowing a child a voice in matters which are the parent's responsibility and a choice wherever it is possible. For example, food and clothing are a parent's responsibility to provide but a child could have a voice. Homework is completely the child's responsibility.

Parents must learn to respond to children with confidence and certainty. Ginott points out that parents in the past always acted with authority while parents today act with hesitation. Two things which help parents be more certain are setting limits on acts and not restricting wishes. Limits need to say clearly what constitutes unacceptable conduct and what substitutes will be accepted.

Counselors can use many of Dr. Ginott's ideas when working with parents or in groups. His methods are not blocked out into a parent education model but they could be used along with other ideas and materials. His work is simply stated and would be attractive for most parents to read.

## RESOURCES

Child Study Association of America, 9 East 89th Street, New York, New York 10028. Has a number of pamphlets and materials appropriate for both parent group members and leaders.

## REFERENCES

Auerbach, A. B. *Parents learn through discussion, principles and practices of parent group education.* New York: John Wiley and Sons, 1968.

Baruth, L. G., & Jones, M. D. Initiating child study groups for parents. *The School Counselor,* 1975, **23,** 121–126.

Berne, E. *What do you say after you say hello?* New York: Grove Press, 1972.

Berne, E. *Transactional analysis in psychotherapy; a systematic individual and social psychiatry.* New York: Grove Press, 1961.

Boroughs, M. C. The stimulation of verbal behavior in culturally disadvantaged three-year-olds through a program of mother-child interaction at home using children's books (Doctoral dissertation, Michigan State University, 1970). *Dissertation Abstracts International,* 1971, **31,** 6890B-6891B. (University Microfilms No. 71–11, 790)

Borstelmann, L. J. Missionaries or educators? Parent education for poverty families. *Community Mental Health Journal,* 1969, **5**(2), 149–155.

Brim, O. G. *Education for child rearing.* New York: Russel Sage Foundation, 1959.

Costello, J. & Binstock, E. *Review & summary of a national survey of the parent-child center program.* Washington, D.C.: Office of Child Development (HEW), 1970. (ERIC Document Reproduction Service No. ED 048 941)

Daniels, R. M. Drug education begins before Kindergarten: the Glen Cove, N.Y. pilot program. *Journal of School Health,* 1970, **40**(5), 242–248.

Donahue, G. T., & Nichtern, S. *Teaching the troubled child.* New York: Free Press, 1965.

Duff, G. H. The impact of pre-school programming and parent schooling on welfare recipient first grade children (Doctoral dissertation, Southern Illinois University, 1970). *Dissertation Abstracts International,* 1971, **31,** 5066A. (University Microfilms No. 71–9985).

Duncan, L. W. *Parent-counselor conferences make a difference.* Washington, D.C.: Office of Education (HEW), 1969.

Fenichel, C. Mama or M.A.? The Teacher-Mom Program evaluated. *Journal of Special Education,* 1966, **1,** 45–51.

Fraiberg, S. Counseling for the parents of the very young child. *Social Casework*, 1954, **35**, 47–57.

Freud, S. *Collected Papers*, Vol. III. London: Hogarth Press, 1950.

Ginott, H. G. *Between parent & child*. New York: Macmillan, 1965.

Ginott, H. G. *Between parent and teenager*. New York: Macmillan, 1969.

Ginott, H. G. Driving children sane. *Today's Education*, 1973, **62**, 20–25.

Glasser, W. *Reality Therapy*. New York: Harper & Row, 1965.

Gordon, I. J. *The Florida parent education model*. Washington, D.C.: Office of Education (HEW), 1968.

Greenstein, B. L., Garman, J. M., & Sanford, J. S. Summer mobile preschool: A home centered approach. *Young Children*, 1974, **29**, 155–60.

Harris, T. A. *I'm OK—you're OK*. New York: Harper & Row, 1967.

Herron, M. Toys can be more than a plaything: Parents in an educational toy lending program. *American Education*, 1972, **8**, 21–24.

Honig, A. S., & Lally, J. *Infant caregiving: A design for training*. New York: Media Projects, 1972.

Jacobs, S. H. Parent involvement in Project Head Start (Doctoral dissertation, University of Texas, Austin, 1970). *Dissertation Abstracts International*, 1970, **31**, 1649A–1650A. (University Microfilms No. 70–18, 256).

James, M. *Transactional analysis for moms and dads*. Reading, Mass.: Addison-Wesley Publishing Co., 1974.

James, M., & Jongeward, D. *Born to win: Transactional analysis with Gestalt experiments*. Reading, Mass.: Addison-Wesley Publishing Co., 1971.

Johnson, D. L., Leler, H., Rios, L., Brandt, L., Kahn, A., Mazeika, E., & Bisette, B. The Houston parent-child development center: A parent education program for Mexican-American families. *American Journal of Orthopsychiatry*, 1973, **43**(2), 206–207.

Johnson, D. L., Leler, H., Rios, L., Brandt, L., Kahn, A., Mazeika, E., & Bisette, B. Houston parent-child development center: A parent education program for Mexican-American families. *American Journal of Orthopsychiatry*, 1974, **44**, 121–28.

Karnes, M. B., Teska, J. A., Hodgins, A. S. B., & Earladeen, D. Educational intervention at home by mothers of disadvantaged infants. *Child Development*, 1970, **41**(4), 925–935.

Koenig, F., Sulzer, J. L., & Hansche, W. J. Mother's mode of discipline and child's verbal ability. *Child Study Journal*, 1971, **2**(1), 19–22.

Kraft, I., & Chilan, C. S. *Helping low income families through parent education*. Washington, D.C.: Office of Education (HEW), 1966.

Lafore, G. G. Practices of parents in dealing with pre-school children. *Child Development Monographs*, 1945, **31**, New York: Teacher's College, Columbia University.

Levenstein, P., Kochman, A., & Roth, H. A. From laboratory to real world: Service delivery of the mother-child home program. *American Journal of Orthopsychiatry,* 1973, **43**(1), 72–78.

McInerney, B. L., Durr, B., Kershner, K. M., & Nash, L. A. *Pre-school and primary education project.* Washington, D.C.: Office of Education (HEW), 1968.

Murphy, L. B., Provence, S., Palmer, F., Gordon, I., Schaeffer, E., Robinson, H. Children under three: Finding ways to stimulate development. *Children,* 1969, **16**(2), 46–62.

Nimnicht, G. P., & Brown, E. Toy library: Parents and children learning and toys. Far West Lab for Education, Research and Development. *Young Children,* 1972, **27,** 110–116.

Ora, J. P. *Regional international project for pre-schoolers and parents.* Nashville: George Peabody College for Teachers, July 1970 (ERIC Document Reproduction Service No. ED 043 179)

Parker, R. K., & Whitney, D. C. A systems approach to early education: The discovery program. *Educational Technology,* 1971, **11**(2), 22–28.

Pierson, D. E. Brookline early education project model for a new education priority. *Childhood Education,* 1974, **50,** 132–135.

Quick, A. D.; Little, T. L.; & Campbell, A. A. Early childhood education for exceptional foster children and training of foster parents. *Exceptional Children,* 1973, **40,** 206–228,

Radin, N. Three degrees of maternal involvement in a pre-school program: Impact on mothers and children. *Child Development,* 1972, **43** (4), 1355–1364.

Rueff, W. N. The effects of a systematic intervention procedure on the styles of mothers teaching a cognitive task to their pre-school age child (Doctoral dissertation, Peabody College for Teachers, 1971). *Dissertation Abstracts International,* 1972, **32,** 3827A. (University Microfilms No. 72–3834)

Sandler, H., Dokecki, P., Stewart, L., Britton, V., and Horton, D. The evaluation of a home-based educational intervention for pre-schoolers and their mothers. *Journal of Community Psychology,* 1973, **1,** 372–374.

Stenner, A. J., & Mueller, S. G. Successful compensatory education model: Pre-school through grade 3. Child-Parent Center Program in Chicago. *Phi Delta Kappan,* 1973, **55,** 246–248.

White, B. L. An analysis of excellent early educational practices: Preliminary report. *Interchange,* 1971, **2,** 71–88.

Willmon, B. Parent participation as a factor in the effectiveness of Head Start programs. *Journal of Educational Research,* 1969, **62**(9), 406–410.

Since many counselors operate from a model most correctly identified as "eclectic," a model is presented that combines elements of several models described previously. This model has been labeled the Solution Oriented Approach to Problems (SOAP). The sources of concepts and techniques within the model are discussed. Counselors are encouraged to develop models to meet their own needs.

*Chapter 7*

# ECLECTIC PARENT EDUCATION*

After reviewing a number of references on parent education, the reader will likely agree with the authors that most practical approaches to parent education do not fit entirely into a single model. A number of concepts are held in common across models. It is also apparent that different terms in the various models can be seen as relating to the same referents in both concepts and techniques. Such procedures as reinforcement (from a behavioral model) and encouragement (from an Adlerian model) appear to be functionally equivalent; we also find proponents of the rational emotive therapy approach using similar procedures. Even though there are a number of counselor educators who feel "eclectic" is a dirty word, experience suggests that once counselors leave their training institutions, very few engage in counseling activities purely within one model.

*The authors wish to acknowledge the contributions of Thomas Reidy in the writing of this chapter and the development of the SOAP system.

The following approach to parent education is proposed as *purposely* eclectic.

The proposed model of parent training was developed by Lamb and Reidy (1975) after they reviewed a number of models and selected those aspects that appeared most useful and congruent with one overall model. It is possible that the proponents of existing models will object to such a combination. Lamb and Reidy used this approach recently and are completing the process of data collection, evaluation and revision. Accordingly, the tentative model is presented to encourage professionals to develop their own models. As long as counselors can support a model with adequate program evaluation, they might as well use the approach most congruent with their specific needs and orientation.

## SOLUTION ORIENTED APPROACH TO PROBLEMS: THE SOAP SYSTEM

SOAP is a way of looking at family life that focuses on the solution of problems rather than on individuals, personalities, and side issues. The problems this method attempts to meet are seen as typical family problems, i.e., when members of the family are unhappy, upset, or uncomfortable about some issue or event. Often families respond in a manner that escalates the difficulties and leaves the original issue unresolved. The steps in the SOAP system are as follows:

   I.   Identification or definition of the problem.
   II.  Determination of ownership of the problem.
   III. Generating several solutions to the problem.
   IV.  Selection of the solution most likely to work.
   V.   Application of the solution.
   VI.  Evaluation of the solution.

## I. *Identification or Definition of the Problem.*

Working with families in a number of settings, Lamb and Reidy found it impossible to solve a problem without some assessment of it. Many times both individuals and families attempt to deal with problems that are either unidentified or incorrectly identified. In a sense, this makes finding an appropriate solution about as impossible as answering a math problem before it is presented. Problem definition is no simple task; difficulties in finding acceptable solutions are often associated with inadequate problem definition. The following guidelines are useful in helping parents define problems:

Type of problem:

1. — Too much of something.
2. — Too little of something.
3. — How to keep something good going.

Description of problem behavior:

Before— What seems to start the action?
When? Where? How often?
Who is involved? Is it usually the same?

Action— What is the action?
Exactly what happened?

After— What happens after the action?
What was the result?
Did anything change as a result of the action?
Was anyone forced to do anything as a result?
Did anyone gain anything?

Be specific and, if possible, talk about observables.
Talk about actions rather than attitudes.

## II. *Determination of Ownership of the Problem.*

Ownership of a problem is important to determine since it often directly affects the definition and limits the choice of solutions. Is the problem really a child's, or is some behavior of the child resulting in a problem for the parent? A child's crying may first indicate that the child has a problem; but if the crying continues, very often the parent develops problem feelings of responsibility or avoidance. Ownership can shift. A child with long hair may not see hair as a problem but the child's parent may describe the child's hair as a problem.

In general, the owner of a problem is the best position to deal with it. Multiple ownership means that several family members share a problem and, accordingly, the responsibility for solving it.

## III. *Generating Several Solutions to the Problem.*

Few, if any, family problems have only one solution. Families must think of several ways to deal with the same issue. Initially, as many solutions as possible should be generated without regard to practicality or appropriateness. Family members may learn something about problem solving by seeing the large number of alternative means of dealing with each issue. It also gives the group a chance to realize that some of the "so-called" solutions could in fact intensify the problem or create new problems. This ability to discriminate, predict, and evaluate is central to problem solving. Parents are urged to encourage children to participate in solution generation. Children's participation is important for four theoretical reasons: 1) if the ownership of the problem is clearly or partially the child's, participation is carrying out the responsibility of ownership; 2) by being part of the process, children are less likely to engage in a power struggle to defeat a solution that is entirely parent generated; 3) since solution generation is cooperative, it teaches cooperating and sharing directly; and 4) participating children observe their parents as models and prepare themselves to use the same methods when they become parents.

## IV.   *Selection of the Solution Most Likely to Work.*

Which of the solutions are unacceptable or impractical? By process of exclusion, the large list of solutions can be quickly reduced. Which ones would set the family up for more problems? These should be discarded without comment about why someone suggested such a "dumb" solution.

Our experience with parents indicates that selecting a solution should involve all family members connected with the problem. Solutions selected by one member of the family or by just the parents are often subject to implicit or explicit veto by another family member. Such an action can be seen as either a mini- or maxi-tantrum, communicating, "You think you're so smart and can come up with a plan to control me. Well, you better have another think because I'm not going along with your fancy plan. What do you think of them apples?" Such a tantrum typically results in a subsequent tantrum by the person who is its object, and the escalation of a war is well underway. Each party brings out bigger guns until one is declared the loser. As we have learned in our work with families as well as from reading historical sources, the declaration of a loser does not always solve the initial problem and often creates a problem more devastating than the original one. (Tantrum—a social interchange where one person has not had his/her needs met and, accordingly, engages in some type of aversive behavior, the function of which is to coerce others into meeting a specific need or to punish them for failure to do so.)

## V. *Application of the Solution.*

The next stop in the SOAP system is to decide when to apply the solution selected in Step IV. It is possible for a family to decide on a solution but to decide further that the solution is not to be instituted until some later point. In practice, many families combine Steps IV and V. Some families decide on temporary solutions to complex problems and continue to use the SOAP system until a more adequate solution is found.

## VI. *Evaluation of the Solution.*

The final step in the SOAP system is the evaluation stage. Frequently when dealing with problems, families fail to assess the results of their work. They move on to other issues without really knowing what happened to the last one. Accordingly, they do not learn from their successes and failures. By systematically evaluating the results of applying the SOAP system to a given issue, families can develop a self-correcting feedback system. If the SOAP system works, they will want to use it again. If it doesn't work, they will need some help from the group and group leaders to make another attempt. This self-evaluation is an instance in which parents can demonstrate family communication and awareness of consequences.

The evaluation of a problem solution depends in part on setting up prior criteria of success or failure. Criteria can be specified easily at any point in the SOAP system, but typically they relate directly to the definition of the problem. If by definition the problem no longer exists and no new problems take its place, then the family members can congratulate each other. If they find that the problem still exists, then they either generate new solutions, redefine the problem, or live with it. In many families this type of evaluation is very difficult since family members often blame each other for the failure of a given solution. Such an adversary procedure is clearly contraindicated since it typically leads to the escalation game mentioned previously. Blaming is not a solution oriented approach to problems. Instead of blame, attention is refocused on the problem.

A. *General format for each session in* SOAP *System.*
1. Discussion of a general topic.
2. Use example generated by leaders (or preferably parents) to elucidate topic discussed.
3. Homework.
4. Feedback—consumer survey.

B. *General format for the entire* SOAP *program.*

Session     I—Description and discussion of SOAP system.
Session    II—Review of SOAP system.
                Topic Discussion: Rules and Requests.
Session   III—a.   Topic Discussion:
                    1. Natural consequences
                    2. Logical consequences—Punishment
                    3. Listening—Playing psychologist.
                 b.   Use of SOAP on problems brought up by parents.
Session   IV—a.   Topic Discussion—Logical consequences—Punishment and Reward
                 b.   Use of SOAP method.
Session     V—Use SOAP method.
Session    VI—Use SOAP method.
Session   VII—Review SOAP method.

## Problems Encountered in Working with Parents in the SOAP System

1.   Father participation. Perhaps the system is threatening or poorly understood or seen as inappropriate role functioning. Pragmatically speaking, fathers may be baby-sitting.

2.   Need to have facility for babysitting other children.

3.   One parent families differ in their needs and capacity to handle problems and implement solutions.

4.   Suggestions for getting parents to participate: reassure them it's not therapy; visit parents in person; send letters, make follow-up calls.

5.   Use school or environment the parent is familiar with for the meeting. This increases willingness to participate.

6.   Dominant members vs. quiet members. Need to draw in the quiet ones to participate.

7.   Be very concrete and use examples parents bring up so the system applies to what they consider "real life."

8.   Problem of parents missing sessions and therefore, some topics. Need to find a way to encourage attendance.

The SOAP system was developed by combining concepts and techniques from various models. Even though Lamb and Reidy were aware that certain parts of the various models were incompatible, they attempted to combine those parts that would complement each other. The general outline of the SOAP system is an almost verbatim repetition of the general outline proposed by Gordon's Parent Effectiveness program. The outline was developed, however, not from Gordon's program but from the standard presentation of the scientific method. The scientific method, or what is known as the hypothetico-deductive method, appears to be the source for Gordon's model.

The specific sections of the general outline of the SOAP system can be traced to other models of parent education. The problem identification section is in a sense represented in all models of parent education. The specific format proposed by Lamb and Reidy is heavily influenced by the behavioral model. The emphasis on observation assessment and the emphasis on determining the events preceding and consequent to a given behavior are clearly behavioral. The section concerning the ownership of a problem was taken from the Parent Effectiveness Training model but would also be seen as congruent with the Rational Emotive Therapy and the Transactional Analysis approaches to parent training. The generation of a number of solutions for a given problem would appear to be common to all models of parent education. The emphasis on including the child in the generation and selection of these solutions appears to be most related to the Adlerian and Client Centered models. The actual change procedure that is selected by a family using the SOAP system is not determined by a given model. In fact the actual technique or solution selected could come from any one or more parent education models. This all inclusive approach to actual solutions clearly defines the SOAP model as eclectic. The evaluation section of the SOAP system is most closely associated with the behavioral model since it returns to the basic data collection approach used in the problem identification section. In short, if the behavior changes, regardless of the source of the technique or model used for bringing about this change, the solution was appropriate.

The example of the SOAP system is only one possible use of an eclectic approach. It is a demonstration of how various components of several models can fit together into an approach to fit local needs and personal styles of the group leaders.

Some problems associated with the use of an eclectic approach are:

1. Lack of readily available material for use by the parents.

2. Lack of consistent theoretical background on which the group leader can rely.

3.  Running the risk of developing a completely idiosyncratic approach to the group that has relevance only to the needs of the leader.

4.  Possible inclusion of concepts that are logically inconsistent.

5.  Consultation and collaboration with fellow professionals is made more difficult.

In spite of these and other possible difficulties, leaders are encouraged to bring in skills and concepts from various models so that the parent education program can benefit from as much input as possible. However, it is possible that one's first group would be both easier and more organized if it were based on one particular model of parent education.

# REFERENCE

Lamb, W. A., & Reidy, T. J. *The SOAP system: a proposed model for parent training.* Unpublished manuscript, DePaul University, 1975.

It is the purpose of this chapter to give a practitioner a set of guidelines and questions to use in preparation for beginning a parent education program in a school.

*Chapter 8*

# GUIDE TO GETTING GOING

The authors recognize that this chapter alone will not completely prepare a person to be successful in parent education. One must be willing to spend time reading the materials which are appropriate to the model selected. In addition, it is strongly advised that specific training in parent education be sought before beginning. This does not necessarily mean returning to graduate school to pursue a list of courses. Alternatives for training include enrolling in a workshop at a professional meeting, arranging consultation with others working in parent education, attending training sessions offered by proponents of a certain model, and working with another professional who has been doing parent education.

In addition the following considerations would be necessary for a successful parent education program:

## I. Steps in Your Own Thinking.

A.  The person who will be the trainer/leader must decide that it is important to be involved in parent education.
  1.  Administration or supervisors should not require counselors to offer parent education.
  2.  Success is likely to be minimal if counselors feel they are not spending their time wisely.
B.  A counselor must decide which model of parent education best fits his/her philosophy and goals.
C.  A decision must be made determining which model can be best accepted by those who are served.
  1.  If the parent population is largely from a particular culture, for instance one in which fathers are dominant, this must be considered.
  2.  If the population is working mothers or single parents this must be considered.
D.  A counselor must be aware of what biases or stereotypes he or she holds toward certain types of families.
  1.  Families from minority backgrounds.
  2.  Mothers with illegitimate children.
  3.  Working mothers.
  4.  Families where fathers make all the decisions.
  5.  Parents who use physical punishment.
E.  One must believe that parents can learn new skills.

## II. Purposes and Goals for Your Program.

A.  Determine what you want to change or achieve, which could be determined in part by a needs assessment of parents.

B.  Determine which population will be served and which model appears most appropriate.
C.  These purposes and goals should be consistent with the goals and purposes of the school curriculum, policies and counseling program.
D.  The goals should be consistent with what the community wants.

## III. Organizational Steps.

A.  Communicate accurately to the administration the purposes and goals of the parent education program to gain their support.
   1.  Point out the positive "spin offs" this program can have in the community, such as a feeling on the part of citizens that the school is helpful to them.
   2.  If parents and schools are cooperating there will be greater success with the students.
B.  Determine if there is money available for materials or whether parents will have to pay. In addition determine if there is money for duplicating materials, films, videoptaping, etc.
C.  Determine if the necessary equipment is available (tapes, tape recorders, videotape, etc.). If this is not available within the school district determine if there are funds for renting equipment or otherwise securing resources.
D.  Determine the best place to meet.
   1.  Specific populations might be more comfortable meeting in homes rather than at school.
   2.  Schools may not have meeting space, so other facilities would then become necessary (churches, park district buildings, etc.).
   3.  If parents have transportation problems, close proximity is necessary.

   E. Identify ways of communicating to parents about the program; usually more than one method is needed. Suggested are:
   1. Community and school newspapers.
   2. Letters of announcement.
   3. Personal invitations.
   4. "Public announcements" over the radio.
   5. Telephone calls by counselors or other parents.
   F. Provide babysitting if needed.
   G. Identify the population you are trying to reach. Criteria for selection may be determined by your purposes and goals.
   H. Communicate the program's purposes and goals to teachers, pointing out how the teacher's job can be more successful if parents are learning how to be more effective with the child. Parent & teachers together can reinforce behaviors like cooperation, good listening skills, etc.

## IV. Some Ideas to Consider.

   A. Opening a Parent Room in the school, stocked with reading materials and other items of interest.
   B. Using plays or drama as a technique.
   C. Structured role playing.
   D. Involving teachers as co-leaders.
   E. Parent education for parents of pre-schoolers.
   F. Co-leading a parent education program with a high school counselor to reach all members of a family.
   G. Using parents as trainers.
   H. Taping sessions for assessment purposes.
   I. Videotaping sessions for parents to view (either those parents who were absent or perhaps those who prefer to not participate in a group).

## Program Evaluation

The general area of measuring the effectiveness of parent education programs has been neglected by proponents of all the models presented in earlier sections of this monograph. The only exception has been the inclusion of what can be viewed as "hard data" in the behavioral model. Since the behavioral model attempts to make the concepts within the model operational it is not surprising to find the goals of observable behavior change used as measures of program effectiveness.

There are basically five types of program evaluation and some that do not exactly fit the categories or combine several of them:

1. Parental reports of their own behavior change or parental reports on child behavior change.
2. Parental reports of attitude or of child-rearing philosophy.
3. Outside observations of behavior change on the part of the parents or children involved.
4. Outside reports of changes in parents' attitudes.
5. Consumer reports from parents.

From a scientific standpoint, taking into account the reliability and validity of observational data, the two approaches in which external observers collect the information used in program evaluation are to be preferred. Baer, Wolfe, & Risely (1968) discuss some of the issues involving research in a behavioral model, and their discussion easily applies to problems faced in other models. Using highly trained observers Zeilberger, Sampen, & Sloane (1968) obtained reliable measures of child and parent behavior. However, from a logistical and simply practical standpoint, the use of highly trained, accurate observers is beyond the resources of most counselors conducting parent education programs. The training, hiring, and constant checking of observers to observe in homes and schools and report behaviors of children and parents in experimental and control groups require considerably more time and funds than are likely to be available to the typical counselor.

In addition to the economic reasons for not providing external observation, the relative lack of observability of the goals of several of the models makes such external observation difficult, if not impossible. Several of the models presented in this monograph make no attempt at making concepts at the level of concrete, observable behavior operational.

Parents have been trained to observe the operational concepts within the behavioral model but there appears to be some question regarding their abilities as observers. Herbert and Baer (1972) demonstrate that parents are not particularly good observers when compared to external observers but point out that even though external observers and parents disagree on specific observations, both can agree on general changes in behavior. Patterson and Fagot (1967) made more typical use of parents in evaluating a training program by administering an adjective checklist and post-parent evaluation to show change. Gordon (1970) presents several parent attitude measures in program evaluation. However, parents may change how they respond to a paper and pencil task closely related to the goals of a program but may not change their behavior with their children. In short, the validity of attitude measures when attempting to measure behavioral change is always in question. Accordingly, the counselor beginning a parent education program is faced with the fact that external observers are scientifically best but usually ruled out by economics of time and money. Parent reports may be of questionable reliability and validity. Attitude measures may not accurately predict how a parent will respond to a real life situation. All of this gives the impression that evaluation is impossible unless the program is part of a funded project which includes collection of research data.

Program evaluation *can* be accomplished in a way that gives feedback to a counselor. Feedback is meaningful if it: 1) aids in making changes that improve a program; 2) aids in identifying parts of the program that should be maintained; and 3) can be used to promote a successful program in the community and school. The consumer reports type of program evaluation mentioned above can readily meet these criteria. Several examples of consumer reports are included in the Appendix following this chapter.

One remaining type of program evaluation not included in the above list may be called simply basic data gathering. The leader of a program maintains information on the following issues to further assist in providing feedback: 1) numbers of families involved; 2) numbers of mothers, fathers, and pairs of parents; 3) types of families represented in terms of size of family, age of parents, economic status, educational background, vocation, types of problems or concerns that brought the family into the program, source of referral, etc.; 4) average attendance and any problems in attendance; and 5) other issues generated by specific interests of the counselor.

Each leader of a parent education group can efficiently gather basic data at the beginning of a group. Consumer reports can be gathered at the end of each session. This information generates feedback and the basics of program evaluation. We feel strongly that *no* parent education program should be run without some form of evaluation. The potential benefits far outweigh the costs involved.


## CONCLUSION

As is apparent, there are a great number of similarities as well as differences among models and techniques of parent training which make it difficult for a professional to decide what is needed for a given program.

We see the following similarities in all the models of parent education presented in this monograph:

1. *Teaching children responsibility* for their own decisions and actions is important to their development. All the models treat parents' inability to allow children this freedom.

2. *Parents must become aware of their own needs* as well as reach an understanding of their children's needs.

3. *Parents must learn to give clear messages.* All models focus on methods of communication to improve parent-child relationships.

4. *Parents must learn to listen accurately and effectively.* Many words are written on parents misreading the child's message.

5. *Parents needs to assess their methods of child-rearing.* It is important to all models of parent education that parents be aware of what hasn't worked in the past and what is possible now. This assessment is important in setting goals for change.

6. *Children are active participants* in that they have learned certain ways of coping with their environment. If these coping mechanisms are seen as inappropriate or unacceptable, parents must make changes so that the children will change.

7. *The earlier the training, the better.* All parent educators agree that early intervention in parent-child relations enhances the chances for success.

Differences reflect the models' theoretical approaches to therapy or counseling. Beliefs about mankind, human abilities and rights and the role of the leader are basic differences. Other differences seen are:

1.  *How much the child has to say.* Some models do not promote the role of child as choicemaker, while others insist that the child play an equal part. Also there are differences in whether children are included initially or only later.

2.  *Goals related to observable behavior or internal processes.* In our opinion all models ultimately deal with both of these. The difference is, in the main, one of focus. This also accounts for differences in how they measure their outcomes.

3.  *Role of the parent educator.* The degree of control the leader exercises in the group or with individuals differs from model to model. The leader may be viewed as an advice giver, expert, group facilitator, or just a listener.

4.  *Techniques vary between and within models.* They range from:
    a.  straight instruction, either theoretical or practical.
    b.  partial instruction and partial role playing, video-taping, shared discussion, etc.
    c.  no instruction, just reflection and listening.

5.  *Child development included* or not included in instruction or discussions.

All parent education models share some of the same shortcomings. Throughout the field of parent education, there are few references on training parent trainers. Exceptions to this criticism are found in material dealing with the Child Study Association of America (which represents a dynamic or psychoanalytic model), the Parent Effectiveness Training program (representing a client centered model), and the Adlerian Family Counseling program. Auerbach (1968) gives a reasonably clear description of the typical training and resultant skills required of leaders working within the CSAA program. Her description, however, gives the impression that actual participation in the training program is the only way to fully appreciate the nuances of philosophy and finer points of technique in the CSAA parent discussion program. The P.E.T. program has a thorough training system set up through the Effectiveness Training Associates which trains and certifies leaders to provide P.E.T. in a manner reflecting the goals of the original program. The Adlerian family counseling program offers a sequential training program that essentially guarantees that trainees completing the courses will have the skills required to provide the services needed within the model. These courses are offered through various Adlerian Institutes which could be located by writing to the American Society of Adlerian Psychology. (Address is located on p. 28 of this monograph) elsewhere in this monograph. Accordingly, at this point, if counselors want to receive training in parent education, they are most likely to find it outside the typical academic training centers. There is no evidence that training in parent education is systematically included in graduate programs.

Another deficit shared by most models of parent education is the lack of specificity in descriptions of actual parent training. All too often examples in the literature read, "The parents were instructed," "The group discussed," "Material was presented," etc. We are well aware that long verbatim accounts of training sessions would be boring and therefore not serve any instructional purpose. However, more detail on specific training procedures would be most helpful to counselors who are just beginning groups. This attention to detail is also a prerequisite to building a research base from which to evaluate the effectiveness of parent education. Without this detail, it is impossible to replicate any previously reported study, and without replication the utility of and ability to generalize from any research are extremely low.

The literature on parent education is also woefully inadequate in matching models to particular target populations. This is similar to the situation of all children coming to a particular counselor receiving the same very specific form of counseling. The children or parents are made to fit the model rather than having the model selected that best fits them. At this point, not enough research has been reported to allow a counselor to assign parents to particular models according to any policy based on empirical evidence. There is a related lack of data for selecting a model for a given setting. In short, counselors will have to continue "flying by the seat of their pants" in this area. Another related area where the research base for parent education is extremely disappointing is in evaluating differential effectiveness of the various models. Accordingly, we suggest that counselors use their own professional judgment in selecting the best model for their situation in light of their own personal skills.

Following this chapter are some sample letters, materials, and evaluations. Do remember to make careful plans for your program and involve important people in your school and community as you progress. Without good planning, proper support, and evaluation you will encounter much difficulty and probably not reach your goals.

# REFERENCES

Auerbach, A. B. *Parents learn through principles and practices of parent group education.* New York: John Wiley & Sons, 1968.

Baer, D. M., Wolfe, M. M., & Risley, T. R. Some current dimensions of applied behavior analysis. *Journal of Applied Behavior Analysis,* 1968, **1,** 91–97.

Beale, A. N. Working with parents: A guidance drama. *Elementary School Guidance and Counseling Journal,* 1973, **8,** 182–188.

Camp, W. L., & Rothney, J. W. M. Parental response to counselor's suggestion. *The school Counselor,* 1970, **17,** 200–203.

Donigian, J., & Giglio, A. The comprehensive family counselor: An innovative approach. *The School Counselor,* 1971, **19,** 97–101.

Downing, C. J. Worry workshop for parents. *Elementary School Guidance and Counseling Journal,* 1974, **9,** 124–131.

Evans, E. Orienting junior high parents. *Personnel and Guidance Journal,* 1973, **51,** 729–732.

Ferguson, G. D. Mother-child interactions as predictors of school behavior (Doctoral dissertation, University of California, Los Angeles, 1970). *Dissertation Abstracts International,* 1971, **31,** 4134A. (University Microfilms No. 71–4869).

Gordon, T. *Parent Effectiveness Training: "Na Lose" program for raising responsible children.* New York: Peter H. Wyden, 1970.

Guerney, B. G., Guerney, L. F., & Stover, L. Facilitative therapist attitudes in training parents as psychotherapeutic agents. *Family Coordinator,* 1972, **21,** 275–278.

Heller, B., & Gurney, D. Involving parents in group counseling with junior high underachievers. *The School Counselor,* 1968, **15,** 394–397.

Herbert, E. W., & Baer, D. M. Training parents as behavior modifiers: Self-recording contingent attention. *Journal of Applied Behavior Analysis,* 1972, **5,** 139–149.

Jacobs, M.; Krueger, A. H.; Lesar, D. J.; & Redding, A. J. Parent perceptions of the role of the counselor in the junior high school. *The School Counselor,* 1971, **18,** 356–361.

Kaczkowski, H. R. An appraisal of role behavior of an elementary school counselor: Summary of a project report. *Elementary School Guidance and Counseling Journal,* 1971, **6,** 5–11.

Kogan, K. L.; Gordon, B. N.; & Wimburger, H. C. Teaching mothers to alter interactions with their children: Implications for those who work with parents and children. *Childhood Education,* 1972, **49,** 107–110.

Kriger, S. F., & Kroes, W. H. Child-rearing attitudes of Chinese, Jewish, and Protestant mothers. *Journal of Social Psychology,* 1972, **86,** 205–210.

Larson, R. S. Can parent classes affect family communications? *The School Counselor,* 1972, **20,** 261–270.

Lillie, D. L. *Parent programs in child development centers. First chance for children, Vol. I.* Chapel Hill: Technical Assistance Development System, North Carolina University, 1972. (ERIC Document Reproduction Service No. ED 067 798)

Niedermeyer, F. C. Parent assisted learning in the inner city. *Urban Education,* 1973, **8,** 239–248.

Norton, F. H. Parental apathy: The school counselor's albatross. *The School Counselor,* 1971, **19,** 88–91.

Parents are people, too.... (H.E.W. Publication No. (ADM) 74–48.) Washington, D. C.: U.S. Government Printing Office, 1974.

Patterson, G. R., & Fagot, B. I. Selective responsiveness to social reinforcers and deviant behavior in children. *The Psychological Record.* 1967, **17,** 369–378.

Schmerber, R. J. Reaching parents through involvement. *Elementary School Guidance and Counseling Journal,* 1974, **9,** 138–142.

Shelton, J. E., & Dobson, R. L. Family-teacher involvement: A counselor's key. *Elementary School Guidance and Counseling Journal,* 1973, **8,** 190–196.

Swick, K. J., & Willis, M. Parents and children in the home environment: Process and product implications for the school setting. *Education,* 1973, **93,** 379–380.

Thoresen, C. E. The counselor as an applied behavioral scientist. *Personnel and Guidance Journal,* 1969, **47,** 841–848.

Worthington, J. A parent's view of school counselors. *The School Counselor,* 1972, **19,** 339–340.

Yarrow, M. R., Campbell, J. E., & Burton, R. N. *Child rearing: An inquiry into research and methods.* San Francisco: Jossey-Bass, Inc., 1968.

Zeilberger, I., Sampen, S. E., & Sloane, H. N. Modification of a child's problem behaviors in the home with the mother as therapist. *Journal of Applied Behavior Analysis,* 1968, **1,** 47–53.

# APPENDIX 1: SAMPLE BOOKLISTS

## Booklists

*Books to Own*—Detroit Public Library, $.50.
Send self-addressed mailing label and payment in check or money order to Publications Department, Detroit Public Library, 5201 Woodward Avenue, Detroit, Michigan 48202.

*Children and Poetry*—Compiled by Virginia Haviland and William Jay Smith, Library of Congress, 1969, 67 pp., $.75. Superintendent of Documents, Government Printing Office, Washington, D. C. 20402.

*Children's Books for $1.50 or less*—Isabel Wilmer, Chairman, Revision Committee, Association for Childhood Education International, 1969, 48 pp., $1.00. A.C.E.I., 3615 Wisconsin Avenue N.W., Washington, D. C. 20016.

*Children's Books of the Year*—$1.00.
   Child Study Association of America, Inc., 9 East
   89th Street, New York, New York 10028.
*Bibliography of Books for Children*—134 pp., $1.50.
   A.C.E.I., 3615 Wisconsin Avenue N.W., Washing-
   ton, D. C. 20016.

## Booklets of Interest

U.S. Government Publications, Superintendent of Documents, U.S. Government Printing Office, Washington,
D. C. 20402.

   *Delinquency Today*—A guide for community action,
   HEW, SES. Office of Juvenile Delinquency and
   Youth Development, 22 pp., $.20.
   *Research Relating to Children*—Bulletin No. 23, HEW,
   SRS Children's Bureau, Clearinghouse for Re-
   search in Child Life, 1969, 161 pp., $1.75.

Child Study Association of America, Inc., 9 East 89th
Street, New York, New York 10028.

   *Preparing Our Children to Live in a World of Diversity by
   Strengthening Their Sense of Identity,* and *Each Child an
   Individual, Promise and Challenge*—$2.00.
   *Current Stresses on Our Children,* and *Impact of the Integra-
   tion Crisis on Children and Families*—$2.00.
   *New Perceptions of Children's Behavior and Needs*—$1.00.
   *The Function of Rebellion—Is Youth Creating New Family
   Values?*—83 pp., $2.45.

Association for Childhood Education International, 3615
Wisconsis Avenue N.W., Washington, D. C. 20016.

*Children and Today's World*—68 pp., $1.25.

*Play—Children's Business*—A guide to the selection of toys and games, infants to 12-year-olds, 40 pp., $.75.

*Discipline*—32 pp., $.75.

# APPENDIX 2: EVALUATIONS

## PARENT GROUP DISCUSSION EVALUATION

1.  The group discussion was worth my time to meet and discuss my role as a parent.

    | 1 | 2 | 3 | 4 | 5 | 6 | 7 | 8 | 9 |
    |---|---|---|---|---|---|---|---|---|
    | | No | | | Some | | | Much | |
    | | Worth | | | Worth | | | Worth | |

2.  This experience has given me a valuable opportunity to communicate with school personnel on an informal basis.

    | 1 | 2 | 3 | 4 | 5 | 6 | 7 | 8 | 9 |
    |---|---|---|---|---|---|---|---|---|
    | | No value | | | Some value | | | Very valuable | |
    | | in opportunity | | | in opportunity | | | in opportunity | |

3. This kind of experience should be provided for other groups of parents.

| 1 | 2 | 3 | 4 | 5 | 6 | 7 | 8 | 9 |
|---|---|---|---|---|---|---|---|---|

No value        Some value        Very valuable
in opportunity    in opportunity    in opportunity

4. (a)  Would you like to have the opportunity of meeting again with this same group?

_____Yes _____No _____Maybe _____Undecided

(b)  Would you like to have the opportunity of meeting again but with another group of parents?

_____Yes _____No _____Maybe _____Undecided

5. I prefer this type of group experience to listening to a presentation by a guest speaker.

_____Yes        _____Maybe        _____Undecided

# APPENDIX 2: EVALUATIONS

## CHILD STUDY GROUP EVALUATION

Name_____

1. Did you attend
   _____(a) all of the ses-
   sions?
   _____(b) most of the ses-
   sions?
   _____(c) very few of the
   sessions?

2. The sessions were
   _____(a) too long.
   _____(b) too short.
   _____(c) just right.

3. The times given were
   _____(a)   convenient.
   _____(b)   fairly convenient.
   _____(c)   not convenient.

4. The groups should be
   _____(a)   more structured.
   _____(b)   more flexible.
   _____(c)   no change.

5. Material covered was
   _____(a)   very helpful.
   _____(b)   sort of helpful.
   _____(c)   not helpful.

6. Did the group experience
   (a)   change your ideas about children?                            Yes____No____
   (b)   change your methods at home?                                 Yes____No____
   (c)   help you to communicate better with your children?          Yes____No____
   (d)   help you to understand the school environment?              Yes____No____
   (e)   change your ideas or attitudes about counselors in the elementary school?    Yes____No____
7. Would you attend these groups if offered again?
                                                                      Yes____No____
8. What did you like best?_____
   _____
   _____

9.  What did you like least?_____

_____

_____

_____

10.  What changes would you recommend?_____

_____

_____

_____

_____

_____

_____

_____

_____

# APPENDIX 2: EVALUATIONS

St. Vincent's Group
Session #_____
Lamb and Reidy 1975

## PLEASE DO NOT PLACE
## YOUR NAME ON THIS SHEET

### *Consumer Survey (or the Nader Report)*

1. At this point I think that these Child Study sessions
   are:

   _____(a)  very helpful       _____(d)  very little
   _____(b)  somewhat                        help
               helpful            _____(e)  not likely to
   _____(c)  I can't tell                    be helpful
                                               at all

2.  This session was:
_____(a)   very helpful      _____(d)   very little
_____(b)   somewhat                         help
            helpful            _____(e)   no help at
_____(c)   I can't tell                     all

3.  The presentations by the leaders were:
_____(a)   not clear at      _____(c)   mostly clear
            all                _____(d)   very clear
_____(b)   somewhat
            clear

4.  To make the next class better, I would suggest_____
_____
_____
_____
_____

# APPENDIX 3: SAMPLE LETTERS

## PROJECT HOME START

WHO: Personnel from Longfellow School
WHAT: A course in child management techniques
WHERE: Oak Park Christian Church (Jackson and Ridge-
land)
WHEN: Monday afternoons, 1:30—3:30
BONUS: Babysitting service furnished

During the school year we invite you to come and share common concerns, ideas and problems with us. The parents of kindergarten children and the parents of primary age children new to Longfellow will be invited to attend one of the courses offered. Our first course will start on October 1 and continue for eight Mondays through November 26.

This invitation in no way indicates that your child is having problems in school. You are invited because we feel that the success of your child in school is very important to you and to him (her).

Dorothy Black—Psychologist

Kathy Fleming—Counselor

Please complete the following form and return it to school by Thursday, September 27.

I will be able to attend_____
I will not be able to attend_____
The number of children I will be bringing for sitter service_____
Ages of children for sitter service_____

_____

Parent's Signature

_____

Phone

# APPENDIX 3: SAMPLE LETTERS

Dear Dad:

We would like to invite you to a series of group meetings along with other dads. The purpose for our getting together will be to discuss the problems of being a father to today's child. We won't be just hearing about what the experts say, but in addition we will share our ideas and learn from one another!

We will plan to meet once a week for eight weeks. The school will furnish all the materials that we will need.

Won't you please check off which time is best for you? We will meet at the Monee Elementary School from 7:30—8:30. We will notify you of the day after receiving everyone's sign-up slip. Hope to see you?

Jackie Lamb, Counselor

Loren Ross, Principal

Monday_____Wednesday_____
Tuesday_____Thursday_____

I cannot attend now but would like to at another
time_____

# APPENDIX 3: SAMPLE LETTERS

SAMPLE PARENT LETTER

(Eclectic Group)

Dear Parents of children at_____:

On_____a number of you attended a_____meeting where a presentation was made by_____. At this presentation a proposal was made to offer a Child Study Course at _____. A description of the course was given and a number of families signed up to be involved in this program. If you signed up at that time, you will be contacted by phone for the final arrangements for starting the course. If you were not at the meeting or did not sign up at that time, this letter gives you a chance to sign up now.

The Child Study program has been presented in other schools in the area and grew out of our contact with parents in these various schools. In working with children, parents and teachers in various schools and agencies, we have been impressed with the fact that many parents share common concerns about their children and families. We have also noted that various families have found ways of dealing with these concerns that can be useful to other families. We have attempted to find a way of helping families deal with their concerns about child management and family communication that can use the solutions developed by other families combined with our own professional background in dealing with children and families.

The Child Study program involves what we see as normal problems or concerns in normal families. All families have difficulties at times. Our goal is to assist families in learning better how to deal with such issues or concerns in such a way that makes the family atmosphere more positive and hopefully decreases the chances of larger problems. We are not attempting to deal with severely disturbed or disordered children and families. We can, however, assist families with more serious concerns in gaining access to sources of treatment in the community.

The program involves a series of ten sessions to be held at the school. These sessions will run from 7:00 to 9:00 p.m. starting on_____. Each session will involve a presentation of a topic by a project staff member, discussion of this topic, and some practice involving that topic. In addition, each family represented in the Child Study program will be selecting at least one area of concern for them and developing a new way of dealing with it. This will involve homework assignments of observation in the home, practice in designing new ways of changing the behavior involved, and ways of evaluating the success of the new plan.

At this point, there are still some spots open in the program. If you are interested in participating, please fill out the attached form and return it to_____.
The only requirements for attending the program are that you be interested in participating and that you agree to an interview with project staff members before beginning the program and again at the end of the project. In this way, the course can be designed to meet the needs of the participants and we can also determine the overall effectiveness of the program by interviewing you after the completion of the program.

Sincerely,

# PARENT RESPONSE FORM

Yes, I am interested in participating in the Child Study program offered through_____. I understand that the program will involve ten sessions that will last for two hours each. The first session is scheduled for_____. I also understand that my family is expected to be interviewed before the first session and again after the last session in the program. I also understand that during the program, I will select at least one behavior in my home that I will work on as an assignment. Please contact me to give me the specific details and arrange the interview.

Name_____

Address_____

Phone Number (Home)_____(Work)_____